CZE
VOICЕ ᔕ

MU01063784

Number Thirty-Nine:
The Centennial Series of the
Association of Former Students
Texas A&M University

CZECH VOICES

STORIES FROM TEXAS IN

the *Amerikán Národní Kalendář*

Translated and edited by

CLINTON MACHANN AND JAMES W. MENDL, JR.

TEXAS A&M

UNIVERSITY PRESS

College Station

Library of Congress Cataloging-in-Publication Data

Czech voices : stories from Texas in the Amerikán
    Národní Kalendář / translated and edited by
    Clinton Machann and James W. Mendl, Jr.
        p.   cm. – (Centennial series of the Association of
    Former Students, Texas A&M University ; no. 39.)
    Translated from Czech.
    Includes bibliographical references and index.
    ISBN 0-89096-471-8 (alk. paper); 0-89096-846-2 (pbk.)
        1. Czech Americans–Texas–Biography.   2. Czech
    Americans–Texas–History.   3. Texas–History–1846–
1950.   4. Texas–Biography.   I. Machann, Clinton.
II. Mendl, James W.   III. Amerikán Národní Kalendář.
IV. Series.
    F395.B67C94   1991
    976.4'0049186—dc20   90-43294
                                                              CIP

Chapter head illustrations are from the 1929 edition of
Amerikán Národní Kalendář.

CONTENTS

Acknowledgments

As our manuscript evolved over a period of several years, we accumulated a number of debts to those who made our continuing work possible. Most importantly, we owe a debt of gratitude to our families for their long-standing indulgence of our stubborn attachment to a field of inquiry dear to our hearts. Ilene Gentry, executive secretary of Research Management at Texas A&M University, was very helpful to us during the early stages of manuscript preparation. The Czech Educational Foundation and the College of Liberal Arts at Texas A&M University provided help at critical times that enabled us to continue our research. The library at the Supreme Lodge of the SPJST in Temple, Texas, and the library at the University of Nebraska at Lincoln were both generous in providing copies of the *Amerikán národní kalendář* for our use, and Joseph Svoboda, curator of rare books and manuscripts at the University of Nebraska, along with historian Bruce Garver, suggested several helpful revisions in the text. We also appreciate the cooperation of Mrs. Thelma Maresh, Marvin Marek, and the University of Texas Institute of Texan Cultures at San Antonio, in providing some of the illustrations.

Introduction

Although the Czechs have been an important ethnic minority in Texas for well over a century, there is comparatively little public awareness of their origins, culture, and place in Texas history, beyond popular associations with *koláč* pastries and polka dancing. In addition, the Czechs in Texas have attracted little interest from scholars (see the bibliographical note). It is hoped that the primary sources made available in the present volume will help to demonstrate the significance of this neglected subject.

During the years of research for our book *Krásná Amerika: A Study of the Texas Czechs, 1851–1939*, we came across various Czech-language accounts by early settlers, travelers, and journalists which offer special insights into Texas and American history. Not only do first-person accounts often given us facts about a bygone age that might otherwise be unattainable, but they record human experiences — impressions, attitudes, emotions — in a way that other sources cannot. For the present book of readings, we have chosen autobiographical narratives written in the late nineteenth and early twentieth centuries that are especially significant because of the writer's identity, his powers of expression, or the importance of the events he records.

Before suggesting ways in which these narratives are representative of the early "Czech experience" in Texas, it is helpful to refer to their unique source. As the subtitle indicates, the selections have been taken from one particular periodical. The annual *Amerikán národní kalendář* (American National Almanac) was published during the long period 1875–1957 by the Chicago publishing house of August Geringer. Geringer was the most important Czech-language publisher in America, issuing the popular daily *Svornost* and the weekly *Amerikán* in addition to the annual *kalendář* and a large number of books. Two of the writers represented in the present volume — Dongres and Buňata — had worked for Geringer, as is evident from their narratives.

The *Amerikán národní kalendář* was by no means the only Czech-language publication of its type in America, but it was the longest-lived and attained the widest distribution. A typical issue contained two to three hundred pages of astrological information and lists of holidays, in typical almanac form; advice; biography and autobiography; popular fiction; poems; recipes; cartoons; descriptions of American laws and customs; short English lessons; advertisements; and so on. Although much of its material had special appeal to midwestern Czechs, the almanac was aimed at a national audience.

Travel articles from Texas were popular, as were short stories and novellas set in that state. Also, the long series of articles entitled "Memoirs of Czech Settlers in America," consisting of short autobiographical narratives, included numerous accounts by Texas Czechs over the years, and occasionally an independent *vlastní životopis* (autobiography) by a Texan would be included. Overall, the *Amerikán národní kalendář* contains a wealth of information for researchers dealing with the history of the Czechs in America. We have chosen ten autobiographical narra-

AMERIKÁN

ROČNÍK   XXIX.

Národní Kalendář

na rok

Sto patnáct obrazků.

1906

Vážný i žertovný obsah.

CHICAGO, ILL.

TISKEM A NÁKLADEM AUG. GERINGERA,
150 West 12th Street.

Title page of the
Amerikán národní kalendář
for 1906.

tives of various lengths by Texas Czechs for inclusion here: Josef L. Lešikar (1880), Josef Šilar (1882), František Branecký (1886), Jan Ustyník (1908), Jan Horák (1929), Josef Lebeda (1880), Josef and Terezie Jirásek (1929), Josef Blažek (1906), Josef Buňata (1936), and L. W. Dongres (1924). Rather than arrange the narratives in order of publication, we chose an arrangement that would best illustrate the evolution of Czech-American culture in Texas in the time periods they covered. The narrative by Dongres is placed in an epilogue because it differs generically from the others. Instead of concentrating on his private life, Dongres, a journalist who in fact conducted the interviews upon which the Jirásek and Horák narratives are based, writes as one who already, in 1924, was concerned with piecing together a history of the early Czech-American community in Texas. Nevertheless, he not only includes some autobiographical details but writes from a very personal perspective, as one who emphatically identifies himself as a Texas Czech.

The narratives chosen for inclusion are interesting for many reasons, but in particular they serve to document the following aspects of early Czech immigrant history in Texas: (1) the record of the earliest group migrations of Czechs to the state, which established patterns followed by later immigrants, as well as various historical precedents set during the early years; (2) key elements in the characteristic way of life adopted by the immigrants, especially regarding their relationship to the land and the development of their own social institutions; (3) the special importance of the American Civil War in the experience of the immigrants; (4) unique qualities of the Czech religious heritage that helped to determine the nature of the Czech-American community in Texas; and (5) the expression and development of Czech ethnic identity in Texas. Each of these aspects deserves discussion.[1]

Among the first Czechs[2] to arrive in Texas were the writer Karel Postl (Charles Sealsfield), who may have visited the Texas-Louisiana borderland as early as 1823; Frederick Lemský, who came in 1836 and played the fife in the Texan band at the Battle of San Jacinto; Bohumir Menzl, a Catholic priest who came to New Braunfels in 1840; and Anthony M. Dignovitý, a pioneering San Antonio doctor and investor who became controversial for his Unionist views prior to the Civil War.[3] These individuals, however, had little direct effect on subsequent Czech immigration.

The Rev. Josef Arnošt Bergman can be described as the "father" of Czech immigration to Texas.[4] Soon after arriving at the community of Cat Spring in Austin County,

1. In addition to these major considerations, the reader will notice various interesting and curious facts that cannot be discussed here. For example, the name of Jan Reymershoffer is mentioned frequently by the immigrants, and he seems to be the principal contact for newly arrived Czechs in Cat Spring in the early years. Josef Lebeda's mention of Czech musicians in Maximilian's army in Mexico calls to mind the problem of the origins of the polka as a popular dance among Hispanic populations in Mexico and South Texas. (The polka is a native Czech folk dance. See Calvin C. Chervenka, "Research Topics Concerning Czech Music in Texas," in *Czech Music in Texas,* ed. Machann.)

2. The term "Czech" refers to a native of the traditional Czech regions or homelands: Bohemia, Moravia, and portions of Czech-speaking Silesia.

3. Machann and Mendl, *Krásná Amerika,* pp. 22–26. Dignovitý himself published (in English) an autobiographical book entitled *Bohemia under Austrian Despotism* (New York: Privately printed, 1859).

4. Blaha and Klumpp, *The Saga of Ernst Bergmann;* Machann and Mendl, *Krásná Amerika,* pp. 26–28.

Bergman began writing to his friends in northeastern Bohemia and Silesia. His letters told of the opportunities that
awaited future immigrants, and provided an important
stimulus to the large-scale Bohemian and Moravian immigration that followed. Josef L. Lešikar's narrative illustrates
the fortuitous nature of the Bergman connection. Lešikar
was an ambitious but poor Czech nationalist who had
given up on his plans to immigrate to Hungary. When he
by chance read one of Bergman's letters about the economic opportunities in Texas he began to discuss with his
countrymen the possibility of a group migration there.
After organizing such an expedition he was, however, unable to convince his own wife to leave her homeland, and
he remained in Bohemia as his comrades left for America,
passing on the leadership position to Josef Šilar.[5] The first
group of immigrants was chiefly made up of poor laborers
from the area around Nepomuky and Čermná in northeastern Bohemia. On August 19, 1851, they began the long,
circuitous journey that would take them to Hamburg,
Liverpool, New Orleans, and eventually, Galveston. Because of dangerous and unhealthy traveling conditions,
only about half of the group's original members, including Šilar, were alive when they reached their final destination of Cat Spring, Texas. The narrative by Šilar's son
(also named Josef), who was only a child during the tragic
journey, graphically describes the suffering of this first
group.

Two years later, Lešikar had overcome his wife's objec-
tions, and he and his family led the second major group
of Czech immigrants, from the same general area of Bohemia, to the same destination in Texas. As he explains

5. Sometimes spelled Šiler, Šiller, Shiller, or Schiller.

in his narrative, however, his group had learned valuable lessons from the earlier one, and their journey was much more efficient and less dangerous. In the following years, the flow of immigrants from the province of Moravia became dominant over that from Bohemia. Two of the Moravians who arrived relatively early are represented in the present collection: Jan Ustyník in 1855, František Branecký in 1856. The route of immigration became progressively better defined and the transatlantic voyage less dangerous; Galveston continued to be the preferred port of entry and Cat Spring the point of dispersal for the immigrants, just as described by Lešikar, Šilar, and the others. The Central Texas counties of Austin, Fayette, Lavaca, and Washington, all mentioned in the early narratives, soon contained important Czech settlements, and Fayette County in particular became established as the center of Czech population in Texas.

There can be little doubt about the primary motive for emigration. Even the self-styled intellectual and political activist Lešikar, with his disgust for the Austrian persecution of Czech nationalists and despair over the elusive reforms that had seemed possible in 1848, emphasizes the grinding poverty of his Bohemian homeland. And the Moravian Branecký's case was typical: after serving in the Austrian army, what was he to do? He knew how to farm, but he had to share a meager inheritance with five siblings. His older brother had immigrated to Texas and reported that good farming land could be obtained there at reasonable prices. In fact, his brother had done so well that he was able to pay for Branecký's passage. Conditions were especially favorable for the emigration of the cottager class (exemplified by Lešikar and Branecký). These holders of small plots of land saw their economic situation grow progressively worse in the second half of the nineteenth century.[6]

About 700 Czechs had established themselves in Texas by the time of the Civil War. By 1900, the number of foreign-born Czechs in the state had climbed to 9,204, and by 1910, to 15,074. After this time, however, decreased immigration caused the number to level off: to 7,700 by 1940, although the number of Czech "foreign white stock" (as defined by the principal language used during childhood) had climbed to 62,680 by that year.[7]

The great majority of the immigrants became farmers, and the pattern of Czech settlements after the Civil War can be directly related to the search for good, new farmland at reasonable prices. Many of the narratives in this book illustrate this pattern of movement, with farm families such as the Horáks and the Jiráseks providing typical examples, and the Ustyníks a more extreme case of the search for better and cheaper land. Even Josef Lebeda, after his exotic career as a soldier in Maximilian's army in Mexico, ends as a farmer in Fayette County.

Most of the approximately 250 Texas Czech communi-

6. See John Chmelář, "The Austrian Emigration, 1900–1914," trans. Thomas C. Childers, in *Perspectives in American History*, vol. 3 (Cambridge, Mass.: Charles Warren Center for Studies in American History, 1973), pp. 342–43. The Czech emigration from Bohemia and Moravia was only part of an enormous exodus from the Austrian Empire. Total Austrian emigration from 1850 to 1914 was over 3.5 million. For more information on the European background of the Czech immigrants to Texas, see William Phillip Hewitt, "The Czechs in Texas: A Study of the Immigration and the Development of Czech Ethnicity, 1850–1920" (Ph.D. dissertation, University of Texas at Austin, 1978), pp. 1–33. Also see Machann and Mendl, *Krásná Amerika*, pp. 9–38.

7. Twelfth Census of the United States: 1900; Thirteenth Census of the United States: 1910; Sixteenth Census of the United States: 1940.

ties that had been settled by the early twentieth century lay within the two comparatively fertile blackland prairie soil regions of the state. The most concentrated cluster of communities was found in the southernmost strip, in an area running from Lavaca County through Fayette County (where Branecký helped to found the town of Praha) and the eastern part of Austin County (which Lešikar, Šilar, and virtually all of the early immigrants who came through the Galveston port of entry had at least passed through) and into Washington County, with a finger running northward into Burleson before trailing off in Brazos County (the home of Josef Blažek). Running roughly parallel to and above this strip was a wider and more extensive strip of blackland prairie, where Czech communities could be found more loosely grouped in a line running northeast from Williamson (where the Jiráseks finally settled down), through Bell, into McLennan County, with smaller, more isolated groupings northward in Hill, Ellis, and Kaufman counties (including some of the area that Ustyník explored before returning with his family to Austin County). Most of the remaining Czech communities lay in the Coastal Prairies region, with significant clusters in Wharton, Fort Bend, Victoria, and a few South Texas counties.[8]

Two basic characteristics of the Czechs in Texas are central to their social structure: the extremely close-knit family unit and the attitude toward the land. Branecký's cooperative farming project with his brothers-in-law is typical, as are Ustyník's odyssey in search of better farmland before returning to the more familiar environs of

8. On the settlement patterns of Czech farming families in Texas, see Hewitt, "Czechs in Texas," pp. 34–71, 104–75. Also see Machann and Mendl, *Krásná Amerika,* pp. 39–70.

Central Texas with his family and Jan Horák's straightforward conclusion to the story of his life: "In 1918 we
bought a piece of land near Fayetteville, and since then,
we have farmed there. Otherwise, our life has gone just
like any other. . . . What more can I say?" The typical
Czech farm family cannot be adequately discussed outside the context of its function as a somewhat self-con-
tained economic and social unit whose main function was
to cultivate the land. The narrative of Mr. and Mrs. Jirásek is perhaps the most representative of all, precisely because at one point the voices of husband and wife become blended in such a way that we cannot be sure which
character is speaking, and near the end we learn of a golden
wedding anniversary, twenty-four *great*-grandchildren,
and the prospect of *great-great*-grandchildren. Farming
was a way of life, not clearly separated from other life
goals and not seen merely in terms of a market economy
as a way of making money.[9]

The matter-of-fact style of the narratives is more likely
to produce interesting facts about the prices of land or
cotton in a certain year than introspective analyses of private experience. Nevertheless, a certain stoical yet good-
humored attitude toward a hard but often satisfying life
pervades the narratives and suggests a great deal about
the nature of life as experienced by the authors.

As Texas Czech community centers were established,
social clubs and organizations began to proliferate, first
on a local, then on a state level, culminating in the estab-

9. Robert L. Skrabanek and Vernon J. Parenton, "Social Life in a
Czech-American Rural Community," *Rural Community* 15 (1949):
225; Robert L. Skrabanek, "The Influence of Cultural Backgrounds
on Farming Practices in a Czech American Rural Community,"
Southwestern Social Science Quarterly 31 (1951): 36–66. Also see
Machann and Mendl, *Krásná Amerika*, pp. 71–90.

lishment of fraternal organizations such as the SPJST (Slovanská podporující jednota státu Texas, known in English
as the Slavonic Benevolent Order of the State of Texas)
and the KJT and KJZT (Katolická jednota texaská and
Česko-řimská katolická podporující jednota žen texaských,
respectively), Catholic-affiliated organizations for men and
women. In each of these examples, the organization grew
out of a nationally based Czech fraternal order, but split
away to become a Texas institution.[10] When Jan Horák
reports that "the first organization" to come to his part
of Fayetteville "was evangelical and came in 1874" he is
probably referring to Česko-slovanský podporující spolek
(ČSPS), a national Czech-American fraternal organization
from which the SPJST split off some two decades later,
the same organization that was so important in the life
of Josef Blažek. L. W. Dongres reports on both the ČSPS
and the SPJST in his narrative.

Dongres also attempts to reconstruct the history of organized Czech-language education in Texas. Bergman was
probably conducting lessons in both Czech and German
in his home at Cat Spring as early as 1855. In 1859, Josef
Mašík became perhaps the first formal Czech teacher in
the United States when he opened his school at Wesley.[11]
The Catholic school built in Bluff (Hostyn) in 1868, with
Terezie Kubalová as the first teacher, may have been the
first of its kind in the United States.[12] Czechs were also
especially active in establishing schools in Lavaca County
late in the nineteenth century. The first school to offer instruction in both Czech and English was established at

10. Machann and Mendl, *Krásná Amerika*, pp. 91–104.
11. Hudson and Maresh, *Czech Pioneers of the Southwest*, pp.
172–73.
12. "Národní svaz českých katolíků v Texasu," *Naše dějiny*
(Granger, Tex.: 1939), p. 242.

Praha in 1870. Although instruction in the Czech language
in the public schools declined rapidly in the late nineteenth
century, Czech-American clubs and organizations continued to advocate the study of Czech, particularly at the
college and university level in Texas. Dongres describes
the persistent struggle to establish the study of Czech at
the University of Texas; it was finally successful in 1915.
(The program of instruction there continues uninterrupted
to the present day.) That language was the most important indicator of Czech ethnic identity is made obvious
by the emphasis placed on it in several of the narratives—
for example, the closing words of Ustyník: speaking of
his children, he says, "We don't have Czech schools here.
But they know how to read and write Czech."

Even a casual reader of the narratives collected in this
volume will notice the prominence of the Civil War in
many of them. The war affected the small Texas Czech
population (about seven hundred in 1861) in important
ways. First, the Union blockade of Texas ports prevented
further European immigration during the period between
1861 and 1866. Second, the war presented those Czechs
already living in Texas with a dilemma: should they join
in the fighting, and if they did not, how could they avoid
persecution? In general, Czechs did serve, but they did not
volunteer for army duty in large numbers. Only about forty
Czechs served in the Confederate army.[13] Most Czechs
preferred to serve a three- to six-month duty in the state
troops or militia. Young Josef Šilar joined the state forces
and helped to capture conscripts who had run away, an
assignment that led to a somewhat ironical confrontation

13. Hewitt, "Czechs in Texas," p. 96; on the subject of Texas
Czechs during the Civil War, see pp. 72–103. Also see Machann and
Mendl, *Krásná Amerika*, pp. 34–38.

with his runaway uncle in an incident recorded in his narrative. The position of the uncle was not atypical of Texas Czechs during the war. Branecký's successful ploy to avoid service is representative. Czechs generally had little understanding of or loyalty to the Southern cause. Very few of them owned slaves—because of their low economic status, because they were committed to an intensive system of farming based on the family unit, and because they objected to the institution of slavery on ideological and moral grounds. Several of the narratives refer to the harassment of Czechs and other immigrant groups during the war years. Most interesting is the case of Lešikar, who was nearly hanged because of his involvement with the (Northern) Czech-American newspaper *Národní noviny*. (His references to German slaveowners should not obscure the fact that as a group the Germans were also widely persecuted because of their suspected disloyalty and abolitionist views.) Although Ustyník's remarkable adventures during the war are hardly typical as a whole, they include three experiences, each of which was shared by at least some Texas Czechs: unenthusiastic service in the Confederate army, escape across the border into Mexico in order to avoid further service, and the decision to serve in the Union army. No doubt the circumstances of publication in the Chicago-based *Amerikán národní kalendář* after the war would tend to emphasize a pro-Union stance in the narratives, but overall the attitudes concerning the war expressed in the narratives are probably typical, especially the pervasive view of the war as a senseless ordeal of economic and physical suffering, and the lack of commitment to the Confederacy.

Another factor was more profoundly affected by the nature of the journal of publication: the pronounced anticlerical and specifically anti-Catholic bias of many of the narratives. In describing his early youth in a village on the Bohemian-Moravian border, Lešikar refers to his mother as a "moderate" Roman Catholic and his father as a strict Protestant, the only one in the village. He writes: "[In the local Catholic grade school] I was held to task even more severely than the Catholic children were, and I was sharply punished for even small doubts in religious matters. For example, when I didn't go kiss the cross . . . and didn't kneel down in the dirt . . . I was bullied by my fellow students. . . ." Later, Lešikar feigned ignorance in catechism class so that he would be judged incompetent for his first communion and thereby be made exempt. Ustyník's childhood memories are similar to Lešikar's: "I attended the Catholic school in Březnice [in the Vyzovice district of Moravia]. In our village there were two Protestant families, father's and Uncle Janoš's, so six of us Protestants went to that school. My father did not want them teaching us the Catholic catechism, so my mother often sent butter and eggs to them so that we would be excused from learning it. . . . The priest used abusive language about Lutherans in front of us. That was a fine way for such a pastor to be preaching!"

Perhaps the most bitter such description is given by Josef Blažek, another Moravian: "Even while I was in school [in Zbejšov u Rosic], I had a great distaste for and mistrust of the priesthood, which became even worse when I recognized how our catechism teacher Hrubeš was deceiving us. In preparation for our first communion he bullied us so about God that I got a headache." Blažek describes his increasing religious doubts and disillusionment with the Church, and in referring to his later life in Texas he sarcastically remarks, "In 1866 I married Josefina Marek, and God has blessed us with three daughters and three sons, so that more atheists were brought into the world."

If one relied solely on the evidence of the religious attitudes portrayed in these autobiographies, one would be inclined to accept the generalization offered by Josef Šilar: "As far as religion goes, there are both Catholic and Protestant Czechs here, but the Czechs are mostly either Freethinkers or nonbelievers." Šilar's statement, published in 1882, is almost certainly incorrect but is interesting in the context of Czech-American religious traditions. In order to understand this context it is necessary to briefly explore Czech and Czech-American history.

Although the early Czech-American press represented a wide variety of political and religious views, a majority of the newspapers and periodicals, including Geringer's *Amerikán národní kalendář,* had a progressive slant and even a bias toward the Freethought movement, an intellectual movement of rationalists and atheists with European roots.[14] Although the last official Austrian statistics classified over 96 percent of the Czech population as Catholic, about 50 percent or even more of the Czechs in America had withdrawn from the Catholic faith by 1920.[15] Although the Czech lands have an ancient Protestant tradition, most of the Catholic losses in the midwestern United States were due to the Freethought movement, which in some areas was highly organized, and to masses of Czech-Americans who simply quit going to church, rather than to Protestant denominations. A few statistics will demonstrate the dramatic nature of this pattern. By 1883, Chicago, site of the Geringer publishing house and home to over 35,000 Czechs, was the most important Czech-American city by far. In that year Chicago had fifty-two

---

14. See Tomáš Čapek's *Padesát let českého tisku v Americe* (1911) as well as the ample chapters devoted to journalism in his books *The Čechs (Bohemians) in America* (1920) and *Naše Amerika* (1926).

15. Čapek, *The Čechs,* p. 119.

Freethought societies, a Freethought school, and only three Catholic parishes. In 1920, 62 percent of the Czechs living in New York professed no religious affiliation. Also in that year, Freethought-oriented bodies claimed close to 80 percent of the approximately 156,000 members of Czech ethnic societies in the United States.[16]

It is clear, then, that the Czech-American population, seen as a whole in the period between 1860 to 1920, was dominated by the Freethought movement. It is equally clear, however, that the Texas Czechs were atypical of the Czech-American population in general during the same period of time. From the 1860s on, the majority of Texas Czechs identified themselves as Roman Catholics. In fact, the percentage of Czech Catholics wishing to maintain their ties to the Church in Texas may have been as high as 75 percent.[17] In 1917, Texas had sixty-eight Czech Catholic "centers" (churches, missions, and stations), twenty more than Nebraska, the state with the second-highest total, yet Texas ranked only sixth among the states in its total population of Czechs.[18]

We can only conclude that Šilar was entirely off the mark in his estimate of religious sentiment among the Texas Czechs and that the strong anti-Catholic bias shown in several of the narratives is at least partially a result of the Geringer editorial policies: that is, the *Amerikán národní kalendář* encouraged a particular religious slant, and non-Catholic readers were more likely to subscribe to and

16. The figures are taken from Karel D. Bicha, "Settling Accounts with an Old Adversary: The Decatholization of Czech Immigrants in America," *Social History* 4 (1972): 45–60.

17. See Machann and Mendl, *Krásná Amerika*, p. 110.

18. Čapek, *The Čechs*, p. 247. The Czech population of Illinois stood at 124,224, while Nebraska had 50,680 Czechs, Ohio 50,004, New York 47,400, Wisconsin 45,336, and Texas 41,080.

read the journal in the first place. (This does not mean that Catholics were entirely excluded from the series of autobiographies in the *kalendář*, however. It is clear from his narrative that Branecký is a Catholic, and Horák seems to be one as well, although neither writer stresses religion.)

There is also another important consideration. Although Catholics outnumbered Protestants among the Czechs in Texas by the mid-1860s, the *earliest* immigrant groups, that is, the Šilar and Lešikar groups, were primarily made up of Protestants from the Landškroun district of eastern Bohemia. For the Protestant minority, childhood experiences from the narratives such as those referred to earlier may have been fairly typical. Because these Czech Protestants came to Texas first, their pioneer status gives their life stories a special interest, even a mythic quality. Furthermore, although Czech Protestants in Texas by the end of the century accounted for only one-quarter or less of the Texas Czech population (with Freethinkers and non-religious Czechs accounting for about 5 percent),[19] the Czech lands have an ancient Reformist or Protestant tradition that is acknowledged even by Czech Catholics. And this ancient tradition resulted in a remarkable ethnoreligious institution in Texas, one that was not duplicated anywhere else in the United States.

To explain this it is necessary to give a few highlights from the complex religious history of the Czechs. The first major, successful Reformed Christian church was founded in the Czech lands a century before the time of Luther. The reform-minded priest and scholar Jan Hus (1341–

19. Bruce Garver, "Czech-American Freethinkers on the Great Plains, 1871–1914," in *Ethnicity on the Great Plains,* ed. Frederick C. Luebke (Lincoln, Nebr.: University of Nebraska Press, 1980), p. 153. In fact, Dongres cites similar statistics in his relatively objective narrative.

1415), who had been influenced by the rebellious English theologian John Wycliffe, was burned at the stake after having been found guilty of heresy by the Church at the Council of Constance. Hus himself had not advocated a break with the Church, but he was considered to be a national as well as a religious martyr, and his death inspired a Czech Reform movement which went through many permutations and changes of direction in the following years. One result was the successful primitivist Christian and passivist movement that led to the establishment of the Unity of the Brethren in the mid-fifteenth century. Although the Czech Reform movement was crushed during the Thirty Years War and officially persecuted by Austrian rulers until 1780, it refused to fade away. And Protestant-oriented Czechs, including many from the Šilar and Lešikar groups, carried the tradition to Texas, where the Unity of the Brethren was resurrected and formally organized as an independent denomination in 1903. In fact, the Unity continues its existence in the state today, very much aware of its Czech origins.[20]

It might be said, then, that Texas is the most Catholic state for the Czech-Americans, but with a significant Protestant minority as well, and an unusually small minority of Freethinkers. For this reason, it is ironic that the Texas Czech autobiographies, which represent such an important regional cultural legacy, have been left to posterity by the Freethought press of the Midwest. It seems less ironic, however, when one remembers the extraordinarily complicated and often paradoxical religious heritage that the Czechs brought with them to the New World.

20. A history of the denomination is found in Christian Sisters Union Study Committee, *Unity of the Brethren in Texas, 1855–1966* (Taylor, Tex.: 1970).

It is not surprising that these narratives, published in a journal read almost exclusively by an audience of Czech-Americans, should express a strong sense of ethnicity. It is not a strident ethnicity, however, and, as noted earlier, language is its chief marker. Lešikar says that he is not bothered by nostalgia for his homeland, as long as he has Czech-language journals to read in America. Occasionally, seemingly casual statements imply the crucial importance of the language. In mentioning his visits to see a countryman named Kříž in San Antonio, Buňata calls the man "a good Czech, but he had a German wife, so his kids didn't know Czech." On the other hand, Dongres (as editor) ends his admiring commentary on the Jiráseks in the following manner: "Their children and grandchildren all know Czech (even now in the third generation), forty-nine sons and daughters of the Hussite nation." Of course, many of these narratives were published before the Czechoslovak nation was created at the end of World War I, a development that led to a marked increase in ethnic awareness among Czech-Americans, as evidenced by organizations such as the Czech National Alliance.[21] L. W. Dongres's narrative in the epilogue, published in 1924, is especially charged with a sense of Czech ethnicity, but, even more importantly for its place in this book, it makes a special point about the uniqueness of Texas Czech culture, again with the emphasis on language.

21. The Czech National Alliance (České národní sdružení), which collected funds to aid the Czechoslovak nationalist movement in Europe, was an outstanding success in Texas as well as in other states with significant Czech ethnic populations, and produced a remarkable book-length record of Texas Czech organizations and cultural activity in *Památník Čechoslováků* (Rosenberg, Tex., 1920). See Machann and Mendl, *Krásná Amerika,* pp. 60–67. This book was edited by Josef Buňata himself.

However naive Dongres's concept of ethnography may be, as a "Bohemian" American he is surely correct in sensing differences in the Czech-Moravian Texas communities that go beyond those of language dialects. Compared to other major Czech-American groups, the Texas Czechs were more rurally oriented in their European homeland, and less susceptible to the disruptions of mass transportation, mass communication, technological advances, and other forces usually associated with urban environments. Small rural communities in a "frontier" area afforded the opportunity of relative isolation. And then the Texas Czechs learned to identify with Texas regionalism, a powerful, romantic identity that was uncharacteristic of most other Czech-Americans. The formerly midwestern, Bohemian-American Dongres has been fully "assimilated" by the time he predicts, as he does in his narrative, that the Moravians of Texas would be the last Czechs in North America to become extinct as an ethnic group.

Translation is always a problematic process, and, needless to say, we met with many difficulties in the various Czech prose styles of the authors. As far as possible, we attempted to preserve the stylistic integrity of the Czech original in our English version. This goal was more easily reached in some cases than in others. For example, Josef L. Lešikar tends to use long, convoluted sentences that simply must be broken into smaller units in some cases in order to make them comprehensible in English. Not surprisingly, the journalists Buňata and Dongres have a more polished style that requires less recasting. In the case of slang or archaisms, we did our best to arrive at modern, English equivalents. If some of the writing seems slightly stiff or stilted, that characteristic may be due to the more formal period style rather than to the difference between Czech and English.

We have limited our use of notes to explanations of words or phrases that are potentially unclear or confusing to the general reader and occasional references that add useful historical or cultural details or cite sources that offer more complete information and analysis than can be given here.

CZECH
VOICES

1 Josef L. Lešikar

Josef L. Lešikar describes himself as "the originator of the emigration of our people . . . to Texas." One might argue that this description could be applied more justly to the Rev. Arnošt Bergman, who began to write enthusiastic letters to his friends and pamphleteers in Europe, urging them to immigrate to Texas, soon after he arrived at the village of Cat Spring, Austin County, in March of 1850. In fact, it was really the combination of Bergman's letters and Lešikar's organizational efforts that led to the exodus of Czech laborers, artisans, and small farmers from an isolated, poor corner of eastern Bohemia to a distant, undeveloped state in the American Southwest.

Lešikar's irrepressible optimism about America, in spite of his troubled life, is one version of the "pioneer spirit" typical of many American immigrants. At the same time, his allusions to his wife's reluctance to emigrate and her ambivalent attitude toward their new home remind the reader of a different perspective. In spite of his meager formal education, Lešikar was a self-taught intellectual and a political activist, caught up in the revivalist spirit of Czech nationalism that was taking place in his homeland. He nevertheless wholeheartedly adopted America as his new home, and he reports nostalgia only for Czech literature.

His autobiography is loosely organized in long sentences and long paragraphs. This style is difficult to translate; occasionally it is barely coherent in the original Czech. On the other hand, it reflects something of the writer's strong personality. Lešikar's anecdote about the edition of the Czech-language newspaper *Národní noviny* that almost led to his hanging just prior to the Civil War became a staple of Texas Czech popular history and appears in Hudson and Maresh's *Czech Pioneers of the Southwest,* as well as other sources.

This autobiography was published in the 1880 edition of the *Amerikán národní kalendář.*

E VEN AS A YOUTH, I OFTEN THOUGHT about leaving behind a few notes about my life for the benefit of my children, in order to warn them and educate them, but until now, my shyness has held me back. Now, however, the requests of several important people compel me to write the following account. Please be lenient in your judgment, dear reader, for all that you will read comes from the pen of an old, ill-prepared man who received no education in his early years.

I was born on the 16th of May, 1806, on the Moravian-Bohemian border in the village of Horbotice, which lies under the political control of the Landškroun district in Bohemia and under the religious control of the Cotkytl parish in the Zábřeský district of Moravia.

My father, Josef Lešikar, was a strict Protestant of the Helvetic Confession. My mother, my father's second wife, was born Rosalie Prokop and was from Crhov. She was a moderate Roman Catholic. This religious difference between my parents was the source of much family unrest

Josef L. Lešikar.
Photograph from collection of
J. J. Stalmach, courtesy University of Texas
Institute of Texan Cultures, San Antonio.

which awakened in me, even in my childhood, all sorts of thoughts and feelings, which, as I now realize, influenced my whole life. When I was six years old, I began to attend the Catholic school in Cotkytl because my father was the only Protestant in my hometown. They didn't make any special provisions in the rules for me like the ones prescribed in similar cases when Roman Catholic children visit Protestant schools. I was held to task even more severely than the Catholic children were, and I was sharply punished for even small doubts in religious matters. For example, when I didn't go kiss the cross which was standing fifty steps from the road, and didn't kneel down in the dirt when the priest prayed that the sick be delivered to the tender mercies of God. For all this and more, I was bullied by my fellow students but would not dare complain to the teacher, Joseph Diblík, who always judged me guilty, nor even to my family. I would not complain, in order to avoid quarrels. I became self-conscious and shy, aided by the inappropriate strictness of my father. I thus lost all of my self-confidence and truly believed that I was the worst child in the neighborhood.

I relate this only to show how an unfair upbringing is destructive for a child. But I'm an old man and recognize the fact that the freedom and spontaneity of which I was robbed as a child will never return.

The cruelest period of my school years came when I was eleven. The teacher picked those students who were competent to go to their first confession, based on their understanding of what is sin and what is not. I was among those included. I didn't know what to do. Go to confession? I would impose the greatest wrath and hate of my father on myself and my mother. I might be expelled from home as a result. And what if I didn't go? I would be persecuted once again by my teacher, the catechism instructor, and my fellow students. So I decided to pretend that I didn't know what a sin was. For example, if I were asked whether it would be a sin for me to steal something from someone, I would answer "Yes." Then to the question of whether I would be guilty of sin if a fellow student stole something and, afraid of punishment, gave it to me to hide for him I would answer "No." And why? Because I had not stolen but instead had protected my neighbor from punishment. "Oh," said Mr. Jupsl, my catechism instructor, "you are very perceptive in other ways; it's strange that you cannot recognize sin." It's possible that he saw through me and speculated about my position. After that, he was not as fanatical as my teacher; I was freed from confession and assigned for the next year. In the meantime, however, a great change occurred. My father sold his peasant holdings and we moved from those sky-high mountains to the town of Napajedla in the region of Uherské Hradiště in Moravia. I attended my last year of school there. The teacher and his assistant were earnest men, and the aged, local dean, Mr. Pátež, and both his chaplains were tolerant. We didn't suffer any unpleasantries from the neighbors, even though we were the only Protestants in the whole area. But we didn't stay there long, though it was good land, because my father was lonely. He was used to a quiet mountain life and didn't like the hustle and bustle of life there. He sold his farm at a loss, and we moved back to the community of Čermenský u Landškrouna to live with a friend of Father's first wife. In time, he would buy another farm. A new, although short, chapter in my life began there. I had the privilege of being Protestant in the Čermenský church, which was of the Helvetic Confession, so I had to prepare for confirmation. I was frustrated, though, because I still had the Catholic catechism in my mind. I wove it into my answers, and it was no wonder, since I had had a Catholic education: yes, I had been baptized, seasoned and anointed with holy oil. When I answered his questions incorrectly, Rev. Gerza used to say, "Well it's obvious that you have studied with the Catholics." But I soon worked it all out and passed my exam with honors. Now my father became concerned with what I should do with my life. From the first, he wanted to send me to the high school (gymnasium) in Modrý, Hungary, where even poor kids could study. He would have had me be a minister or preacher, but at the school they determined that I should be a tailor. I'm not going to describe all my experiences as I entered this new field; I'll just say that I passed all the exams, from grade to grade, which every novice must take if he wants to reach the rank of journeyman.

When I was seventeen, my father died, after an active life. Now my mother wanted me to take up religion again, thinking that it would broaden my horizons, give me a wider field of opportunity. But I felt much freer as a Protestant, much as a nobleman who is free from serfdom and the *robota*.[1] So I remained a "ram," as people say. Soon after my father's death, I received my diploma as an expert tailor. Then I gathered my knowledge along with my possessions into my bag, and said goodbye, and went to Hungary. I lived through the most beautiful and happy times there. Also I came to know a little political freedom, for they had a constitution in Hungary at that time. I would have stayed there permanently, but the notary in St. George stamped my work papers through Brno, back to Landškroun, when I wanted to go farther into Hungary. He said that I didn't have permission to travel there.

---

1. *Robota* was a law that bound the peasant to work free for his lord a specified number of days each year.

So I saw my mother again after an absence of two years, and I had a good outlook, as long as I didn't receive a white uniform with ornaments, for which I had very little desire. At that time, it was easier to avoid the draft if a man was married, so it made sense for me to get married, in order to avoid military service. Married life, on the whole, has been very happy for me, because my wife, who up to this day is like a blessing from heaven, has always been considerate, diligent, and faithful to me. With her I inherited a little place (measuring a little less than nine *měřice*).[2] We had to live very modestly because neither the farm nor my work as a tailor earned much money. (I must confess here that throughout all my experiences, I've never been unhappy; I have always been satisfied with my position, and satisfaction is true wealth.) Unexpected aid came to my limited position. The Nepomuky community, where I lived, named me notary public, with an annual salary of ten *zlatý*, each of which would be worth about two of our dollars today. As is known, besides this there was also payment in kind; it was then down to worries. Someone might say: "Ninth trade, tenth poverty." I don't want to argue about it, for it could be true.

New worries began as a result of my office, how to fulfill the duties expected of me. Like most young people, I had forgotten the things I had been taught. I even had to learn how to write my own name properly. Well, necessity is a great teacher. Even the magistrate of the village did not know how to write. There was very little printed in Czech for us to read. All official business, written in German, by law came to me, since I was being paid by the community. The magistrate had only to make three crosses for his signature.

2. One *měřice* is equivalent to half an acre.

These circumstances provided much good practice for me, and I must say that in a short time I made remarkable progress. I didn't want to fail to come up to par. My farm and business suffered because of it, but I gained knowledge. I read good books from wherever I could dig them up—mostly German but a few Czech books—except for those about religion. You just couldn't find those in the countryside in those days. I especially liked the philosophy of Freethought. The religious difference between my parents was the motivation for that. I longed to discover where the truth was. Until then I had been leaning toward Protestantism, but how astonished I was when I came across the book *Ruinen der Städte von Volnay.* I read a lot of Blumauer, including *Das Glauben und Wissen,* Hegel, Schlegel, and many others.[3]

As I said, there had been no Czech periodicals during that time. The first I was able to find was *Květy,* a literary journal. At the same time, I was able to obtain a copy of *Slávy dcera* from someone studying in Hungary, and I was very happy to see that ardent patriots still existed. Now I progressed fearlessly and quickly, down the road to freedom of the spirit and body; I happily broke the shackles of the spirit. It's not easy to get rid of these heavy burdens. It takes a lot, especially for a man like me, who has to pick up his convictions like spilled poppy seeds, but a strong will comes to the forefront. The memorable year of 1848 inspired me even more. I didn't hide my convictions when I campaigned in my region for the election

3. Johann Aloys Blumauer (1775–98; the original text has *Blaumauer*) was a former Jesuit known for his controversial, radical attacks on the Catholic church. Today his works are difficult to find. Georg Wilhelm Friedrich Hegel (1770–1831) was one of the most prominent German philosophers. Carl Wilhelm Friedrich von Schlegel (1772–1829) was an important German literary theorist and critic.

to the Czech Parliament of the candidates from the regional committee, L. Šlesingr, from Ustí nad Orlicí, and Rybička, a doctor from Česká Třebová. I called meetings in every surrounding village, and everywhere the people told me, "We don't know these men." There was no use in pointing out this fact to the committee. I lost heart. You could see that our National Revival was lost, because the Germans were united in power.

Election day came, and the *vikarius* of Landškroun announced the candidates.[4] Among others, a certain Václav Lešikar, from among us there at Nepomuky, had supposedly declared himself a candidate. I knew that was a lie and an insult, because nobody from around there had that name. It was shown that no one from among us with that name could have been announced as a candidate, and I insisted that the *vikariát* tell me who had given him that name. For a long time his excellency was reluctant to do so, for he was one of those dyed-in-the-wool Germans. Finally he said that a certain Stránský from Řetov had suggested that person. I don't know how it happened, but in all four voting districts of Landškroun, I received the most votes. But I can honestly say that I hadn't actively contended for it, and I hadn't even thought much about it. After me, a certain farmer named Václav Pešl, who was a German and a stand-in for Šlesingr, and Rybička, were elected. As everybody knows, the Czech Congress did not meet, because Windischgrätz had already bombarded Prague by that time. Still, I must say a few more words about the preceding referendum of the Frankfurt Assembly, by which Austria was supposed to become the glue to hold together the tiny German states, mainly as a bul-

4. This official was a Roman Catholic clergyman (vicar) and his office was known as the *vikariát* (see text following).

wark against Russia. Of course, no one from a Czech village showed up for that vote. And as for the German voters, I was able to show those upon whom I had some influence that Landškroun would not be well served by the vote. With all of this, I really annoyed Baron Vojt, the regional commissioner in Chrudí, who had been sent to supervise the referendum. He summoned me to a private inquisition and asked me why I was making such a fuss about the vote. I would have to be quiet about it, if I valued my life. In that fast-moving time, I had the opportunity to meet many outstanding personalities, either in person or through correspondence. For example, there were Božena Němcová, Klácel and other ardent and honest patriots, the future parish priest of Česká Třebová (is he still alive?), and Bedřich Košut, Arnold, and many other members of the former "Svornost." As a result, when the German reaction set in, I became known as a "Svornoster."[5] Of course, I was under police surveillance, and a gang of *gendarmes* were daily visitors. They even awarded me with visits during the night. A corporal named Šrenk was especially intrusive. He was always asking me what the government was doing (more than once, I wanted to reply that it was getting in debt over its ears). When he asked me to show him which books I was reading, I set in front of him *Bruncvík, Meluzína, Jiříkovo vidění,* a dream book, and *Selská Pranostyka,* which a certain old lady had lent to me. I spent a lot of time in this way. I subscribed to *Národní noviny, Šotek,* Havlíček's *Selské noviny,* and *Večerní list* from Arnold. In addition, I received the *Česko-Bratrský Hlasatel* from B. Košut, and I openly read this and others, especially *Moravské noviny,* which the noble

5. The term *svornost* (unity) gave its name to this Czech patriotic society.

and good Klácel, at the request of Božena Němcová (with whom I was in frequent correspondence), sent for three years free of charge.[6]

I progressed a great deal at that time in a spiritual sense, but my material position was always limited. I felt sorry for my wife, who had to put up with so much trouble, but married life was like this for many in our area, due to our faithless government, during the breakup of the Imperial Parliament in Kroměříž. Up until then, I had supported the empire, but what was I to do now? Where was I to go? I felt pressure from all sides. I knew something about free America, but the question was, how much money would it take to get there? For similar reasons, many others in our village at that time were thinking of immigrating, mainly to the Banat region of Hungary. I didn't agree with that idea, however, because of the unhealthy land in that region, the crude and uneducated people there, and, finally, because, after their unsuccessful revolution, the Hungarians hated the Slavs and Germans and would give them all kinds of trouble.

My warnings might not have been convincing, had not a copy of a letter by a certain Protestant minister named E. Bergman fallen into my hands by chance. Bergman had emigrated from Stroužný, Prussian Silesia, to Cat Spring, Texas, and had written from there to a man by the name of Kalačný, one of his friends in Stroužný, advising him

---

6. This list of people and publications demonstrates Lešikar's acquaintance with Czech intellectuals and writers of the time. Most significant are Božena Němcová (1820–62), the first major Czech woman writer and author of the classic novel *Babička* (Grandmother), and Karel Havlíček Borovský (1821–56), the first independent Czech journalist. Lešikar's eroding support for the Austrian Empire, expressed in the following paragraph, is typical of Czech nationalist thinkers at this point in history.

to follow. He described the cost of a trip, outfitted by Valentin, from Hamburg to Texas; what kind of food and services would be available on board the ship; what the countryside was like over there; and the people and how they made a living. I told those who wanted to go to the Banat about the letter and that I had decided to move my family to Texas. I was going to apply for a passport and sell our little farm, but my wife did not want to leave her home village for an unknown country overseas. Since I didn't want to force her to move, we stayed on our little place. The other sixteen families embarked for Texas in the fall of 1851 from Hamburg. It was the first emigration from eastern Bohemia and Moravia, and nobody knew whether any Czechs at all had gone to America earlier, because the government carefully suppressed all news of immigration to America. They also placed all kinds of restrictions on it. In Hamburg, our poor emigrants fell into the hands of a Jew named Hirman, who gave them a contract via England to Liverpool. But there they were given another contract. They received uncooked food, moldy and rotten, and every family had to cook for itself. Their ship, the *Victoria,* was already crowded with Irish emigrants. Because of these conditions, half our emigrants died during the seventeen-week voyage.

For almost a whole year we heard nothing about our unfortunate countrymen. Only in September of 1852 did we receive the bad news of their sad fate. And then the correspondence began. In the meantime I had been corresponding occasionally with our dear Klácel, mainly about emigration. He continued to encourage me, and I was able to pass on everything to him so he could publish it in his newspaper. That way someone who was going to make the passage could find out about current conditions from someone who had firsthand experience. So Bergman's letter was published word for word in the *Moravskě noviny,* which Klácel edited. In this way, news about Texas in America was spread all over Moravia in detail. The result was a general emigration from eastern Moravia to Texas, from Vsetín, Vyzovice, and the area around there. So I consider myself the originator of the emigration of our people from here to Texas, and I don't think anyone can challenge that.

In 1853, my wife finally decided to emigrate, for the benefit of my grown sons. It was difficult because my oldest son was already over the age of twenty and thus liable for military service. This was troubling because he would not be allowed to go to America. However, due to the intervention of Count Norbert Poeting of the Landškroun district, a good friend of mine, he was judged unsuitable for service by the military doctor and released.

Now it was full steam ahead. Seventeen other families prepared to go with us, and on the 9th of October, 1853, we left our home. At the beginning of November, we boarded the ship *Sava,* on which we had to wait for fourteen days in Grag, and on Christ's birthday we arrived in Galveston. Our voyage across the ocean lasted about seven weeks. On the whole, it was pleasant, and the supplies from Bedeker in Bremen were good enough. We considered ourselves lucky compared with those who had gone before us. After a short stay in Galveston, we were taken by steamboat to Houston, and from there into the interior by slow-moving oxcart. (There were no railroads at that time, and Texas was not like it is today.) The trip lasted fourteen days and was about sixty miles long. So our complete pilgrimage lasted about fourteen weeks. We finally came upon the remnants of our suffering countrymen near New Ulm. Several of them were working there. About four families had hurriedly built a log cabin in which they lived collectively. It had burned, however, and they had lost everything that they hadn't lost on the trip. Yet their spirits hadn't fallen. They were hopeful about the future, and almost all of them eventually became prosperous citizens. My wife was not at all pleased by the trip to Texas and the meeting with our countrymen. She grew silent and melancholy; however, I found comfort in freedom. We found employment for our children, and my wife and I lived with one of our friends, who, after the fire, had built a rather shabby cabin. He was Karel Šiller, who now lies in his grave. May he rest in peace. In 1854, a certain Czech-German fellow and I bought an unfinished farmstead and we lived together on that godforsaken place for two years.

In truth, it was not an enviable way of life, so we divided the land, and I got the part without a building or cultivated land. I started to do carpentry work with my two oldest sons, and by Christmas of 1856, I was under my own roof. Everyone knows that things are always hard in the beginning. I experienced this in the extreme: my partner and I had been swindled out of about seventy acres of the farm we had bought, and we owed a great deal on it. Due to lack of money, I bought a Mexican pony for riding, and he threw me off whenever and wherever he pleased. One time, he almost killed my wife. I bought a team of oxen, one of which was already entertaining the thought of passing from this world, and soon did go to see his father. Many things such as this happened to me during a very short period of time. The needy one always buys at the highest cost, especially when he buys on credit. So, when all is said and done, I got along at a snail's pace, but at least I got along.

As I said before, in those days Texas wasn't like it is today. Nice buildings were not to be seen, only log cabins, which did not contain a single nail. In place of windows there were only holes. A door was knocked together from some pieces of wood or some kind of fabric. Boards and other necessary items were scarce. In our whole settlement there was only half a wagonful. It was many years before I was able to get that kind of material. But during that time I didn't for one minute get homesick for my former homeland, because that would have done neither her nor me any good. The freedom and liberty here cheered me up, for I wasn't one of those many people who, I would say, are immature, who are always holding on tightly to their mother's apron strings and screaming, "Mother, Mother, Our Mother!" Still, even today, I honor and respect my native country. Really, though, I've always been satisfied here, even in the cruel times of the Civil War. My situation has always been improving, and I haven't missed anything except our literature. I didn't even hope to live to see that sort of thing in America. I didn't know, though, that such a large number of our countrymen lived up north or that an active Czech press existed. All of a sudden I got a letter from Jan Bárta Letovský, who, I recall, was one of the first pioneers, telling of the Czech literature here. I still don't know how he found out about me in Texas, for we had never seen or heard about each other before. He told me that he was working on a campaign to start publishing a Czech newspaper up north. That was "Joy in Israel!"[7] I rounded up twenty shareholders in my area, and soon the first edition of *Národní noviny* came from St. Louis. I was named their chief agent in Texas.

However, they began imprudently and uncautiously. As a legal stockholder, I saw what consequences that might have and felt that an additional policy was needed in or-

7. See 1 Chronicles 12:40.

der to ensure the success of our newspaper. I advised that if they wanted to preserve our *Národní noviny,* it would be necessary at the beginning to stay out of controversy, to restrain political as well as religious opinions, in order to hold our people together, whatever their professed views and whether they identified with the free or the slave states. But it was all in vain. Abraham Lincoln was announced as candidate for president in bold headlines under Old Glory and his complete program was described. That, and my name as agent, led many Americans and Germans to sniff it out. There were even some countrymen who, despite my warnings, let the slaveholders know what was in the paper. Then my persecution and suffering began. I was denounced as the worst kind of abolitionist. The English and German newspapers publicly announced that I and Jan Reymershoffer,[8] from Cat Spring, who had also become an agent for *Národní noviny* by that time, must be hanged from the nearest oak tree. I was constantly afraid for my life then. Once about six of "the boys" came to see me. They were mainly Germans, and their leader was Arnost Knole. I met them with my head held high. Indeed, I had nothing to feel guilty about, and I got out of that mess all right.

I must add here, however, that the local Americans remained surreptitiously vigilant, but were not nearly as vicious as many of the German slaveholders were. It was a cruel time. Later on, even some of the Germans who were not necessarily abolitionists but only loyal Unionists were imprisoned, and many of these were even lynched. The uproar caused by the war was at its height then. Texas was cut off from the rest of the world, and there was no way to escape except through Mexico; and even that was

8. In the original text, Lešikar misspells the name as *Reymerhofr.*

Jan Reymershoffer,
an early resident of Cat Spring,
who is mentioned in several of the narratives.
Photograph reproduced from Hudson and Maresh,
Czech Pioneers of the Southwest.

very difficult to do. Everyone who could carry a weapon, without exception, had to go to war—from age eighteen to thirty-five. And, finally, up to age fifty. The older ones were forced to volunteer as so-called "minutemen." There were hardly any white people around, except old men with gray hair, women, and children. Every male was under arms. They had to leave their land because of the war, and the war effort drained away their tax dollars and fodder, cotton, corn, and bacon. They summoned three of my sons together, declaring them volunteers. I finally freed the eldest, saying that he was past draft age. He had to serve in the militia, however. They would have caught the youngest one, but I went to General McCrudy and explained that he was not yet eighteen years old. He went to Mexico out of fear, and the poor boy died there as a result of tortuous work. So all three sons were taken from me. In addition to this worry, other cares occupied me, such as my farm work, my wife, and the family of my oldest son. But there was something still worse. My two middle sons, who were enrolled in the regular army and had been encamped for a time at Brenham, were ordered to fight in Vicksburg, Mississippi.

I can't describe the state of my heart as I saw them off. I envisioned their wounded bodies, or even their corpses, which they were being forced to sacrifice to the preservation of slavery and the destruction of the Union. I can't describe the emotions which ruled over me at that time. Three days after my sons left, Tomáš and Jan Votýpka, the two sons of my neighbors, joined the parade. It was a terrible mess. How can you hide from such a ferocious pack of wolves? Indeed, as I said earlier, because of the Czech newspaper, I was hated as a dangerous abolitionist, and it was clear to me what was going to happen. The end of the war was nowhere in sight. In fact, I was afraid that slavery would win out in the end, since English business interests gave it their financial and moral support. As the war raged around Vicksburg, our boys escaped injury, but when Vicksburg fell, the Confederate soldiers were captured. When they promised that they wouldn't fight against the Union any more, they were released to go home. The faithless majority of them immediately formed a regiment under a different name to fight against the Union, and they tried to force those who didn't want to fight anymore to go along. Then they started to hunt down those who didn't want to fight for the Confederacy.[9] The bands of hunters wandered day and night across the countryside. They conducted their hunt as if they were after wild animals, with dogs that had been used to catch runaway slaves. A pack of these hounds fell upon the wife of one of my sons. They tore at her dress and she would have been terribly hurt if help had not arrived in time. If this mob ever recognized a horse, saddle, or anything else belonging to the one they were hunting, they simply took it for themselves.

Most of all, they liked to invade a residence at night and turn it inside out. I was treated to a good number of these visits because I was a reputed abolitionist. I was always afraid for my life. "Master Lynch" reigned supreme. My sons and their friends had to stay in the forests, hiding in the hollows of trees and thickets in both summer and winter, and in the rain, which is quite substantial here. They were barefoot and ragged; there wasn't much of anything that you could buy. Goods didn't arrive in Texas unless they came through Mexico, and they were very expen-

9. At this point, Lešikar includes the reference to a note (omitted here) that summarizes the major historical events leading to the Civil War.

sive. A simple woman's apron cost thirty dollars, a pair of slippers fifty dollars, and boots one hundred dollars. But a pound of cotton brought only seven cents, and in Confederate currency at that. You had to sell your cotton to the government, because England traded the rebels' cotton for arms and other war matériel through Mexico. We had to wean ourselves from drinking coffee and eating pastries made from flour. We were very temperate in those days, but the Americans were a little better at it than we were. The black women and the older Americans knew from the old days how to weave cloth and dye material of all sorts. The blacks produced leather and made their own shoes. In this way, they were able to provide the most necessary items. I can't describe what we experienced during those three years. Among other things, we were sure that if the Confederacy prevailed, all immigrants would have their property confiscated and that we would be driven from the land. People were shot at as though they were dogs. Once they shot at my son, but they missed him. That's all that I was able to find out about it. All of this happened in a very short period of time, relative to one's life, but it seemed like eternity to me before I heard any more about him. I thought he was hurt very badly, but, luckily, he escaped serious danger. However, Tomáš Votýpka, my neighbor's son, was shot and taken to jail, where he died, to the grief of his parents. But then came an even sadder catastrophe: their other son, Jan, was also caught and sentenced by a military court to death by a firing squad. Before the sentence could be carried out, however, he escaped, and he is alive and well today.

It's difficult for me to write any more about that horrible time—by no means have I run out of material. Let me just add that we got out of it in good health, and that is unusual, considering what we went through. Only once

my son did get jaundice and had to be treated by a doctor.
But was it advisable to reveal his hiding place or even his
disease? In my distress, I found out about a certain doctor who would willingly give medical aid to anyone, even
if he had to go secretly into the forest. So I went to him
seeking help, and that noble humanitarian willingly gave
it to me without saying a word about it. He was concerned
only with curing disease and caring for suffering people.
He didn't care about the circumstances. My thanks and
praise go out to this honorable man. He is Dr. Nagl, who
now lives in St. Louis. Everything in the world has an end,
and the unexpected news that the rebels had been completely defeated came all at once. The war was over. It
was such a surprise that I couldn't believe it at first. Indeed thoughts from my childhood of the time Napoleon
was defeated came to mind. I warned my sons that they
shouldn't be too quick about getting back into the world.
I wasn't able to return to a secure life for a long time. I
looked around me and saw the world as a child sees it
for the first time. I longed to hear something about my
native country and to read Czech newspapers printed in
America. For a whole year we had heard no news other
than the victories of the rebel forces. Slowly we began to
revive, both spiritually and materially, for after the war,
the price of cotton climbed to fabulous heights. It brought
up to thirty cents a pound in good money. (In the course
of the war, Confederate money fell to the value of one cent
on the dollar, and finally it wasn't worth the paper it was
printed on.) Many who had raised cotton in wartime and
had had to keep it themselves suddenly became wealthy.
I even made some money off cotton, enough to recover
from the old setbacks. So this verifies the proverb: "Some-
body always profits from a war." Just as the sun is lovely
when it breaks through the clouds, so was the coming of

peace to me. Although I had suffered a great deal and had lost about two thousand dollars' worth of produce, during that time I had never regretted coming to America. And I declare from my heart that in spite of all this I never for one moment yearned for my former homeland. Well, there's nothing special in the comfortable circumstances of life, and whoever has not suffered doesn't feel the full achievement of freedom and can in no way measure its advantages and properly esteem or know the price paid for it: for example, the free blacks around here.

Now I'm sitting peacefully with my wife in our happy family circle, with my remaining three sons, their wives, and fourteen grandchildren. I get along well with my neighbors and the multitude of [Czech] national journals affords me instruction, pleasure, and a wide view of the world. I'm glad that I've lived in such a significant era, and I have the hope that, whether today or tomorrow, I will leave the scene of this busy life of mine in peace and contentment.

2 Josef Šilar

Yielding to the pleas of his wife, J. L. Lešikar did not leave for Texas with the first group of emigrants from the Landškroun region of Bohemia, which he had helped to organize in 1851. He was fortunate, for the ill-fated 1851 expedition provided the Czechs with valuable experience that would make the second expedition in 1853, which included Lešikar and his family, a much less dangerous undertaking.

Leadership of the first group fell to a craftsman named Josef Šilar,[1] and his then thirteen-year-old son by the same name is the author of this account of the 1851 journey and the group's subsequent experiences in Texas. It was published in the 1882 *Amerikán národní kalendář*.

Šilar's story suggests both the extreme suffering of his group (only half of whom survived the journey) and the wild spirit of adventure felt by a young teenager. Like Lešikar, Šilar provides anecdotes about the Civil War and how it affected the recent Czech immigrants. Czech settlers in Texas were relatively isolated from

---

1. The spelling of the surname *Šilar* is that given in the original text, but the name commonly appears in historical texts and legal documents in various forms: Šiler, Šiller, Shiller, Schiller.

each other as well as from the majority population at this time. Overall, the density of the Czech population was simply not sufficient to support a large, well-organized ethnic community. The total Czech population in Texas was under one thousand until the 1870s.

Šilar presents an extreme example of how the experiences of immigrants can change from one generation to the next. Neither his father nor his mother survived for long in the new land, but he went on, in spite of setbacks, to lead a successful life, becoming the second Czech (after Antonín Haidušek) to receive a law degree in Texas. It is interesting to note that Šilar, like Haidušek, was an assimilationist who set out to develop business and personal relationships with Anglo Americans. He even married an Anglo woman.

IN 1851, A LARGE GROUP OF CZECHS FROM Nepomuky set out on the road for Texas. Among them were my father Josef Šilar and his family of three children.[2] They went from Liverpool to New Orleans and were in transit for ten weeks. They had a very bad trip because they were weakened by disease and badly cared for on the ship. Over half of them had to go to the hospital in New Orleans after they landed. My parents, brother, and sister were all taken there, and only I remained with my uncle Ježek in the hotel. Only a few of the travelers knew German and none knew English, and since there were no Czechs in New Orleans, we couldn't converse

---

2. The wife of Josef Šilar, Sr., was also included, although the phrasing does not make that fact clear. In the next sentence, the author speaks in the third person, although he, of course, is included in the group.

Josef Šilar,
at the age of eighty-four.
Photograph reproduced from Hudson and Maresh,
Czech Pioneers of the Southwest.

with anyone. In fact, I was only semiliterate in Czech, for I had been to school for only a few months with Mr. Mašík in Čermná. I was only thirteen years old then. A few days later I went to visit the members of my family, who were lying in the hospital. Not being able to tell anyone what I wanted, I had to wander around the hospital, trying to find my loved ones. When evening came and the sisters had seen me wandering around, they took me to supper, let me wash up, changed me into clean night clothes, and put me to bed. The patients around me were constantly screaming, so I couldn't sleep. About midnight, I got up and ran downstairs to get out of there. The hospital was surrounded by a high fence, and all I could hear was the wailing of the patients and the barking of the dogs outside. I wanted to go through the gate, but it was locked. Without pausing to think it over, I climbed over the gate and happily ran into the street where everything was dark. It was about three miles to uncle's hotel and I wandered through the streets of the city, chased by the dogs, not knowing what to do. Finally, as dawn was breaking, I found the hotel.

After awhile those travelers who had not died were released from the hospital. Now we went to Galveston, where more of us got sick and some died. The same thing happened in Houston. From there, we were hauled on wagons to Cat Spring. It was in the spring of 1852 when we came to the Brazos River, which was flooded and about six miles wide. We made camp there and stayed fourteen days. We found some fruit there which resembled nuts. Some ate the nuts, but the fruit was poisonous, and everybody who had eaten it suffered terribly; a few died as a consequence. We stayed in Cat Spring awhile, and I went to study with a certain German, while my father and the others soon moved to Industry, where they are still living. My father bought some land there and paid it off, but did not see to it that the purchase was entered into the title abstracts. After settling there, my father sent me to a certain American who taught me English. While I was still there, in 1854, my dear mother died, and my father came to tell me the sad news. However, another cruel shock awaited him, for no sooner than he had returned home, his house, along with his deed and everything he had, burned up. Father now brought his older son back home and began to re-build, but before he could finish he died too. We were placed under the guardianship of Mr. Ježek, but he soon died as well, so we three children had truly become orphans. People advised us to ask the previous owner of the land to return our money rather than try to get a new deed from him, so we did just that. The former owner gladly fulfilled our request, and in a short time our lost money was restored. At that time, land was cheap here. For two dollars per acre we were able to buy land that now costs ten to fifteen dollars. In my spare time, I was learning to read and write English, and in 1885, I quit working and went to an English school. Looking for a way to make my living in the world, I entered into a closer relationship with the Americans. I recognized the advantages of their political system. They took a liking to me, and it happened that I became an overseer of slaves for which I was paid three hundred dollars a year.

In 1861, an expedition from our town to Durango, Mexico was organized. It was made up of 140 people, men, women, and children, and all the participants had the highest hopes of finding a lot of gold and silver. I was among the participants. We had wagons and all the necessities with us. We had been on the road a full three months when we arrived at Cornetto Los Indios. Captain Box Bill was the leader of the expedition.[3]

When we arrived, we had neither money nor livestock, because they didn't get one blade of grass on the entire trip, and they died on us. When we got there we found out that Captain Box had a contract with the governor of the state of Durango. If he led us there, he would get twenty leagues of land. We had been completely deceived. Silver was to be found there, but in hard rock, and we were in no way equipped to get it out. So the whole group set out on the return trip. On this trip they always hitched a horse and mule together to one wagon and they did the best they could to get as far as possible. Smallpox broke out and we had to lay fourteen members in the cold ground.

As far as I am concerned, I can say that I liked it in Mexico very much, because it has a healthy climate, like that in Bohemia. And the soil is so fertile that any other people besides the Mexicans, who are terribly lazy, could earn great wealth from it.

I returned to Texas, my new homeland, in September, 1861. I didn't want to go to war, but, seeing that I would soon be forced into it, I went to volunteer and was put in the cavalry, in the so-called "Patriotic Regiment." Our general thought so highly of us that he never sent us out of the state. I was in Brown's Company, and our duty was to catch all "conscripts," that is, men who were called to duty but ran away. Czechs were very often found among the runaways, for their wives didn't want them to leave home and family for the war. They didn't have anything to fight for. They weren't afraid of losing their freedom,

3. This is the name of the captain as it appears in the original text. Perhaps the given name and surname had been transposed.

and they didn't have any blacks as slaves. These conscripts usually hid in the woods, where we were sent to find and capture them. Our company was stationed about two miles from my uncle's house. I knew that he was hiding in the woods, and where. Since I hadn't seen him for a long time, I went to visit. When I arrived at his farm, it was evening, and he had just come out of the woods. He greeted me in the usual way and asked what I was doing. When he found out, he said, "I'm a conscript, too—what are you going to do with me?" I answered, "Dear Uncle, let me stay with you overnight, since I haven't seen you in a long time. In the morning, I'll return to my company. Then I will get back to work and do my duty, searching for conscripts. If I find you, Uncle, I can't help it, we'll have to take you to camp." Uncle answered, "Well, stay here the night, son, and tomorrow go do your duty. As for me, you can be sure that I will not let you catch me." The next day we went after my uncle but couldn't find him. I could write a great deal about the Czechs hiding in the woods and about the misfortunes suffered in the war, but space does not permit. After the war, I settled in Eagle Lake, where I farmed one year with the help of some blacks. But after losing six hundred dollars in cash, I decided to open a business. That was in 1867. At that time, an American named Thomas Parmer moved to our town. His family is one of the oldest in Texas, for they settled here in 1824. Parmer had an attractive and honest daughter, and now she is my wife. In 1875, my health worsened to the point that I had to sell my store, and so I started to study law. I received a law degree in 1877 and since that time have continued to practice that profession. There are only two of us Czech lawyers in Texas; the other one is Mr. Haidušek in La Grange. I predict that the Czechs and Germans will someday have the best land in Texas, because they keep buying, whereas the Americans are always selling.

As far as religion goes, there are both Catholic and Protestant Czechs here, but the Czechs are mostly either Freethinkers or nonbelievers. In the schools they teach in English and German, English and Czech, or all three languages.

3 František Branecký

The story of František Branecký is typical in many
ways. He was part of the early stages of Moravian immigration to Texas, arriving early in 1856. Like many
other immigrants, he was trained in a craft but saw few
opportunities for making a good living in his homeland. Farming in Texas seemed to be an attractive alter-
native. His description of the "immigrant experience"
during the Civil War is typical, and so is his record of
struggle and hardship before settling down as a successful farmer and raising a large family. Finally, his
joint venture with two of his brothers-in-law, although
it is not fully explained, is characteristic of Czech farmers of the time.

Branecký helped to develop the town of Praha (originally Mulberry) in Fayette County. Because of the
town's name (Praha, or Prague, is the capital of Czechoslovakia) and its later importance to the Texas Czech
community as a whole, Praha is called "*Matička Praha*"
(Mother Praha) even today. In spite of the fact that it
has nearly become a ghost town, it is still the site of
one of the largest and best-known annual Czech festi-
vals in Texas.

Branecký's autobiography appeared in the *Amerikán
národní kalendář* of 1886.

I WAS BORN ON THE IST OF DECEMBER, 1821, in the village of Lišná in Moravia, near Přerov. My father was a farmer. When I was twenty-one, they drafted me into the army. I served in the first regiment of the Austrian infantry in 1848 and 1849. Fortunately I survived the war, serving with Marshall Radecký in Italy. I was in the army a full nine years before I was discharged. What was I going to do now? I was trained as a weaver, but the trade wasn't going very well at that time, and so, since I knew how to farm, I took a job with a farmer. My parents had died when I was thirteen years old, and because there were six of us children, I didn't inherit much; also, I was the youngest. My entire share of the inheritance was about eighty *zlatý*.[1] I soon grew weary of my work and, more and more, felt a desire to immigrate to America. Just in that same year, 1855, several families were setting out for America, and I prepared to go with them. One well-to-do farmer, F. P., tricked me into going by saying that he would pay my passage over and that I could work for him. He said that I would have it good with him. I believed him, and so we left our dear native land. On the 8th of October of the same year, we boarded the ship in Bremen, and on the 3rd of January, we arrived in Galveston. We went from Galveston to Houston by the bayou, and in Houston two farmers, Mr. Helsher and Mr. Knipscher from Ross Prairie and Fayet ville, loaded us onto wagons. They had taken their cotton to market, and they carried us to Cat Spring. We paid them one dollar for every one hundred pounds. We traveled from Houston to Cat Spring in twenty-one days by oxen. At that time the town wasn't much more than a prairie and a heavy forest

1. At the time of writing, one *zlatý* (literally, *gold piece*) was equivalent to about two American dollars.

that was full of wildcats. When we came to a well, our baggage was dumped and we were told that this was Cat Spring. We thought that there was supposed to be a town, but there was only a farm, which belonged to Mr. Reimershoffer.[2] He took us under his roof so we wouldn't have to find other housing for ourselves.

He had me cutting brush and herding his stock, for which he paid me thirty cents a day. Of course, that was very little pay, but in those days the blacks had to work for nothing. They were slaves, and so there was no need for day laborers. Then I went to work for Mr. Egkinek at Millheim,[3] where I was employed for one month. After that, my sponsor and fellow immigrant F. P. bought a farm; he came to me and said that he needed me very much. He tricked me into going by saying that he would pay me well. He also said that he always would divide things equally with me. I went with him, but it turned out badly. I was with him for two years, and the money which I had brought with me had run out. Finally, I told him that we should settle up because I had grown weary of working for him. He did not fulfill his promise. He considered me a slave, and he told me that I was indebted to him and that he didn't want to give me anything. I brought charges against him before a judge in Columbus, but I lost. I should have gotten $162.00 from him, but I lost the case and still had to pay him $17.00. His lawyer had arranged it all so that I had to lose. He even counted little items that F. P. had given me earlier, like a piece of chewing tobacco or a little whiskey, and charges for laundry and such, even for a plow that had broken on me, although it wasn't my fault. All of this was read to the judge,

2. Usually spelled *Reymershoffer.* See Lešikar's narrative.
3. The original text has "Vilheim."

and I was mad, but I couldn't do anything about it. I was just relieved to find out that I didn't have to pay more, and that is how we parted.

Later I became a sharecropper, for in those times there wasn't any other way. I was there for one year and that was bad, too. With what I had earned I bought a cow and a horse, but thieves stole everything from me. The next year I went to work for ten dollars a month, but, unfortunately, I got very sick. I had pneumonia and was laid up for seven weeks at a countryman's place. When I got well, I walked to Houston, where I ran into Mr. Květoň. He offered me a job and we worked together in a brick factory, where we made two dollars a day. That was fine, but it didn't last long. After we burned up a kiln, we were out of work. Then we started hauling oysters from the boats to places all over the city. I stayed for fourteen days, but only Irishmen were there. I found work on the railroad which went from Houston to Allentown. There I made four hundred dollars in two years, but today I'm still holding a note for one hundred dollars of it, and sixty dollars was stolen by our boss. I lost patience with that kind of work, but I was happy and didn't worry too much about it. Finally, I packed my bags and wandered back towards Frelsburg and Mr. Pivoňka's place. There I happened to meet a widow with a young child. I took her for my wife and began married life, supporting my family. I had two hundred dollars to start with, and she also had quite a bit of money, as well as a few head of cattle. I thought that this might be a more peaceful and satisfying life, but I was mistaken. The Civil War broke out the next year, and our peaceful life was over. The rebels pursued every man from eighteen to fifty and forced them all to join the army. Although I was not that old yet, I told them that I was past fifty. They didn't want to believe me, and I had to go in front of a judge to prove it. Then I had to go to Columbus to have a general affirm it. There a doctor looked me over, even at my teeth, as you would a horse. I insisted that it was true, and then the general said, "Let him go; he's an Austrian soldier, anyway, and he'll just give us trouble." Then he signed my papers and I was out of it for good. I must point out how the soldiers treated us. The rebels took a third of everything the farmer had, including fodder for animals and food for people. Mostly they took it from the Czechs and Germans because they went along with them. It was very bad for the farmers. You could hardly buy anything, from clothing to food. Everything was very expensive, and the tiniest thing cost a dollar. When I had gathered my cotton, I was again afraid that the rebel mob would take it away from me, and so I hid a bale in the forest, in a remote spot. It's impossible to describe how bad it was for immigrants at that time. But it is always clear after the storm. The war ended, and then came the golden times, when we could breathe freely. During the war, cotton sold for three cents a pound, so it was hauled to Mexico. After the war, it rose to thirteen cents, and then to twenty-five cents. I got twelve hundred dollars for my cotton that year because I had some hidden back. But when I added up everything I had only a few hundred dollars, because I had some debts to pay off. I looked for something to buy with the remaining money. I set out with a friend and we went west, to High-hill in Fayette County, and then to Mulberry. Then, at the place where Praha now stands, there were forests on both river banks and a farm stood on each side of the river. We stopped at one of them, where a Czech named Novák lived, and then we bought the other farm, which belonged to an American. He gladly sold the farm to us for four dollars an acre, and then we three brothers-in-law divided it.

We had a lot of trouble getting everything in order. But it all worked out, and now I live happily with my big family, my wife and ten children. I married off two daughters just recently. At the beginning it wasn't good in Mulberry. We didn't have a church or a school. In order to go to church, we had to travel to Hallettsville, twenty-five miles away. We asked the priest over there, Father Fares, if he could come to our town sometimes, and he agreed to hold services at the Nováks' house every fourth Sunday. A couple of years after that, we built a school, and now we already have built a third church and a second school, more substantial buildings than the first ones. Now the Texas Praha is thickly settled, and the former peace and quiet which we used to have here has been interrupted by a lot of disorder. There are a lot of rowdies who are used to fenceless range. Every farmer has fenced his property, and they go around cutting people's fences. They don't let anybody alone. But we also have some good young people here. Well, everywhere there are cockleburs among the wheat.

4 *Jan Ustyník*

Though he was over twenty years younger than his fellow Moravian Branecký, Jan Ustyník arrived in Texas with his family slightly earlier, in 1855. Also in contrast to Branecký, who apparently was a practicing Catholic, Ustyník was a member of the Protestant minority in his homeland, and his autobiography, like some others in this collection, refers to Catholic persecution.

When Ustyník's autobiography was published in the *Amerikán národní kalendář* of 1908, the editor noted in an introduction that it was "rich in detail." The author's recollection of people and places and facts such as land prices in a particular locality and year adds to the historical value of his account. Beyond mere factual detail, Ustyník's story further illuminates aspects of the Czech immigrant life that have been described or suggested by the other autobiographers: attitudes toward the Civil War, the dangers and rewards of life in a relatively unsettled area (in this case, a curious mixture of frontier hospitality and fear of violence and crime), and the constant search for better and cheaper farm land.

Though Ustyník's style is typically straightforward (occasionally spiced with humor), his story includes active service — and desertion — during the Civil War, travels in northern Mexico and the midwestern United States, and other adventures that make it entertaining reading.

The original text was printed in a single paragraph. Paragraph divisions have been added.

I WAS BORN ON JUNE 6, 1842, IN KUDLOV, in the Vyzovice district of Moravia. Father was a farmer, having about 120 *měřice* of land in several scattered plots,[1] and on each plot was a small wooded area. He had two oxen with which he plowed while I harrowed and broke up the clods with a hoe. He didn't have any horses, but he had three cows, some hogs, and about forty sheep. For that farm, as I remember, he got about six thousand imperial crowns.

I attended the Catholic school in Březnice. In our village there were two Protestant families, father's and Uncle Janoš's, so six of us Protestants went to that school. My father did not want them teaching us the Catholic catechism, so my mother often sent butter or eggs to them so that we would be excused from learning it. In the summer we didn't go to school. I was glad, because the priest used abusive language about Lutherans in front of us. That was a fine way for such a pastor to be teaching! I learned a little reading, writing, and arithmetic, but when I left school I was only a little better off than when I began. So then my father sent me to Zádveřice for an education. I was there four weeks and that was all. I couldn't put up with the whippings I got, not because I was disobedient, but because I didn't learn the catechism.

After that we moved to America. In 1855, my parents

---

1. One *měřice* is equivalent to half an acre.

Jan Ustyník.
Photograph reproduced from
the *Amerikán národní kalendář*, 1908.

immigrated to America with four children — I, my brother, and two sisters. After eight weeks on a sailing ship, we reached Galveston, Texas, and following a short rest we went on to Houston in a small steamboat. Since there were no railroads at that time, my father and those with him were forced to obtain wagons for the long trip to Cat Spring. About three wagons traveled together, and it took eight days. We didn't have much to eat because no one had known that we would be traveling through such a wilderness where nothing is for sale, in fact, nothing is available. Those who had guns shot some kinds of birds, and when we spotted a farmhouse we would run up to it, asking for something to eat. But those poor folks usually had little for themselves. We had many adventures during the trip. Five to six Texas oxen were hitched to each wagon, and only children rode on the wagons — the adults walked. And when the oxen got stuck in a mudhole, the children were carried to dry land and the wagons were pulled free with great effort.

And so toward the end of June we arrived at Cat Spring. We boys had imagined it to be some kind of town, but there was only one business — Mr. Reymershoffer's.[2] We camped there, some under the trees, others in Mr. Reymershoffer's yard.

Now the building of a home became the main concern of my parents. My father, Jan Ustyník, along with Josef, Petr, and Jan Mikeska, went to Industry, and there father and Josef Mikeska bought a farm from F. Knole, making a down payment of two hundred dollars. Since we owed money on the farm, Knole gave us a place in the stable to live, and both families moved there in July of 1855. We carried wood on our backs and cooked outside. We had

2. Ustyník spells the name *Raimeshoffer.*

only two pots, one tin bowl, and a few forks. Our fare was corn bread with gruel, three times a day. In the mornings we had black, bitter coffee. A person could not get fat on that kind of diet. Worst of all, there was no work to be had until fall, when they would start to pick cotton. Around Christmastime, both families moved out to the farm, and both lived in the same building, an arrangement which didn't work out well. Mrs. Mikeska constantly longed for the Old Country, and my mother wanted to see her brother again in Cat Spring. Knole was asked to take the farm back. He agreed but kept the two hundred dollars and allowed us to make a crop that year. My father worked thirty acres and gathered twenty-five bushels of corn and one bale of cotton, for which he got sixty-five dollars. We planted the seed corn too close together, and the corn was so thick that not even a chicken could walk through it. We all got sick that year, and one of my sisters died. She is buried in the Methodist cemetery in Industry. The illness prompted us, especially Mother, to think of returning to the Old Country. But that would not be possible any time soon.

That fall my father sent me out to work for Mr. Reymershoffer at two dollars a month. I served only two months because, after that, there was no more work to do. So, I walked the fifteen miles home with my four dollars and the gift of a new hat on my head. During the Christmas season, a German moved to the farm, and he asked my father to send me to work for him at thirty-six dollars a year. Father agreed, and when my parents moved to Cat Spring, I remained with the German. He was a poor tenant farmer. He had only one horse, a pair of oxen, and a wagon. The oxen ate the corn straw that we had left there and I felt sorry for them, but I didn't have it much better. The German was extremely pious; he prayed and

I had to pray with him. As long as there wasn't much work, it was all right, but when the work started, I was often hungry. Nevertheless, I stayed with him six months, but once when he and his wife went out visiting, I gathered up my few rags and left to find my parents in Cat Spring. I wouldn't have made it there if I hadn't been strengthened by a dinner at Petr Mikeska's home along the way.

By then my father had moved to Millheim, to the farm of his brother-in-law Josef Skřivánek, and he agreed to break up the prairie, fence it in, and work as much of it as he wanted. Again, there were two families living in one building, with no forest, so father bought from Mr. Kuna twenty-five acres of prairie land which included about two acres of woods. He erected a hut, or rather a sod house, and moved there in the same year. It was about a mile from the Skřivánek's, and when I came home my parents were already living in that hut. Father wasn't happy that I had run away from my job, but when he saw my miserable face he didn't say anything. He contacted Mr. Lešikar about asking the German for my pay. The man didn't want to hear anything about it, but finally he gave father an old brass watch. I was glad that it was all over. I traded the watch for a pistol, but as soon as I had shot it a few times, it broke, so I had nothing to show for my half year's work. That was in 1857. My sister, who was two years older than I, had been working for Mr. Nagl. My brother, who was two years younger, and my little sister were still living with my parents. Because of that, I went to work for Mr. Kůň. He was Czech, and I had it good there. He paid me four dollars a month.

Also at that time my brother had gone to work for a German but had stayed with him only a day, and that same German asked father if I could work for him. Father wanted to buy some wooded land from him, so I had to do it. I stayed there for eight months. At first I got six dollars a month, and for the last four months I got eight dollars. By the time I went home, father had one horse, a pair of oxen, two cows, twenty-five acres of prairie land, twenty-five acres of forest, and a house.

In the year 1858 a brother was added to the family, but he died and is buried in the cemetery at Millheim, where other Moravians who traveled with us on that sailing ship also rest. They were from Želichovice, Lípa, and Zádveřice. Old man Trčálek was among them, along with his wife, his son and son's wife, and their two children. They had bought thirty-five acres of land and built a house on it, cutting all the lumber themselves. But a year and a half later old Trčálek died, and in 1859, the other four died. They are all buried on that property. Of the two orphaned children, the boy was adopted by a Koch near Bellville, but I think that he died. The girl was taken in by a German. To this day she lives in Cat Spring but she has probably already forgotten her mother tongue. Mr. Kuna got the land back. Trčálek had paid him but he did not have the deed, so the descendants could not claim it. At least that's the way that I've always heard it. The Trčáleks were a respectable family.

At the beginning of 1859, father bought a wagon and two pairs of oxen on credit, and, with my brother and me, began to farm. We fenced in fourteen acres and rented sixteen more. We gathered nine bales of cotton and quite a bit of corn. Father paid for the wagon and the oxen.

In 1860 I went to work for an American named Swearing for one hundred dollars a year. I was glad when I was able to buy a horse for sixty dollars. When I returned to my parents, my brother and our brother-in-law Jan Štefek were renting land. He had married my sister in 1859 and lived in Travis County.

At that time, the Civil War broke out. When my brother came home to the family in 1862, I enlisted in the 22nd Infantry, Company A. Our commander was Captain Daniels. In Ezel Grove [sic], two miles from Hempstead, I took my oath and then was released for six days in order to find a weapon. My father had brought a shotgun from Moravia, and he gave it to me. The blacksmith made me a long knife, and I was ready to be a soldier.

When I went on guard it seemed as if I were stepping on wild geese. There were twelve hours of duty, and each man stood duty for two hours and then rested for four. The enemy was over one thousand miles away from us, of course, so we didn't have our shotguns loaded. During the day no guards were posted, but at night everyone had to know the password. One night it was "Daniel" [sic], the name of our captain. The soldier whom I relieved told me that anyone who could not tell me the password should be shot. Of course, I didn't see how I was supposed to do that if my shotgun wasn't loaded. At ten o'clock, the corporal came to trade places with me, but I stopped him and wouldn't let him approach. He thought I didn't know what I was doing, and only when I drew back the hammer did he jump back. He called for the day officer, but I stood firmly in his way with my empty shotgun. Only when the guard with duty after mine said to let him pass did I agree, and that was out of fear. As the reader can see, we were really well-trained soldiers.

We stayed there for three months, until the order came to prepare to board the train for Sabine Pass. They said that twenty thousand Northern soldiers were there and that we had to give them a licking. We left our shotguns behind, and in Houston we got some old rifles with straps. Then they ordered us to bake enough bread for three days. Since I didn't have anything else for this purpose, I used an old pot that the chickens had been drinking out of. Prepared in this way, we moved toward the enemy by train. That evening we reached Beaumont and made camp. Then the search for food began because we had eaten up everything we had brought for the trip. The people were reluctant to sell us anything because soldiers usually forget to pay, so the majority of us went to bed with empty stomachs. On the next day we received the order to load our guns and wait for the enemy, but they apparently had gone back to New Orleans. The truth is that twenty-two Northern ships had sailed into Sabine Pass unnoticed by the town until two of the ships ventured farther up the channel. Then the fort opened fire on them and they surrendered. During this incident, it became apparent that our gunpowder was no good. Not one round had reached the enemy, and yet the army was now ready to take the field.

We were ordered back to our old camp, and the procession to the train was undertaken with more enthusiasm than had been shown in the attack upon the Yankees. Nothing special happened on the trip back to Houston except that the soldiers ate up the dinner that had been prepared for the employees of the train. In Houston they led us to an enclosure ringed by a strong guard so that no one could get out. For supper they gave us each a piece of bacon and six biscuits. In the morning we boarded the train and were taken to Camp Gross.

We had remained there for about a month when once again the alarm sounded that twenty thousand Northern soldiers stood before Galveston. The train flew down the tracks, and at four in the morning we were already at the creek where Cook's battery of heavy artillery lay. A regiment of cavalry also arrived. When dawn broke we spotted the Northern ships in the harbor and then moved the majority of the inhabitants out of the city. We camped about nine miles from Galveston, and there we got new rifles and good cartridges. I was the only Moravian in the regiment, but there were four Bohemians, the Štapl brothers and the Koláčný brothers.[3] They were in the band. In Cook's regiment there was one Bohemian, and when he found out about us, he came to see us. He was our drummer. Our food there was bad, and we had little water. We got corn bread and lean beef.

About a month before Christmas in 1862, our company moved to a spot about five miles from Galveston to guard the island, but not once did we come close to the city. I really wanted to get into the city because I didn't like fighting against the Northern army. However, I was not successful. We were lying in foxholes and there was also a battery of artillery with us. Two Moravians, the Šebestas, and one Bohemian, J. Mašek, served in that unit. Then on Christmas Eve a messenger arrived with the news that many boats full of Northern soldiers were coming and that they were preparing to attack us. That very night, we were ordered to dismantle the artillery; then the train came, and we loaded everything on it.

By morning we were nine miles from Galveston, having torn up the railroad tracks and rolled up the telegraph lines behind us. In our new position we learned that there was only a small contingent of Northern soldiers at Galveston. In the new year, several of our regiments arrived, and we were still preparing for the march to Galveston. The soldiers themselves pulled the heavy cannons and placed them across from the port. A big ship with eight cannons was anchored in the harbor, and several small ships, also with cannons, were riding on the waves. Not

3. See the essay by L. W. Dongres in the epilogue for a discussion of Moravian, as opposed to Czech, identity.

far away were two sailing ships with supplies. At Pelican
Spit,[4] about three miles from the harbor, there was a war
ship, and a few companies of Northern infantry were stationed there. That was the entire armed might of the
Northerners. There were about ten thousand of us Confederates. At that time, two ships from Houston arrived
and they ordered about two hundred soldiers on board,
each of the men receiving twelve empty bags. I was among
these "baggers."[5]

We were taken to Fort Point and there we positioned
two cannons and then filled the bags with sand in order
to build ramparts. The enemy started to bombard us after
midnight, and our heavy artillery answered them. Now
it became dangerous to build the ramparts because of the
bombardment and so you hid wherever you could. When
dawn broke we could see a ship coming from the direction of New Orleans. Her cannon roared and a round
landed behind us. The second one was a little closer, but
before the third could land, every one of us was on the
run. Several soldiers were killed and several wounded. During the retreat our soldiers threw down their rifles, food,
and even extra clothing.

When everything had grown quiet, I returned to town
and found bread and meat strewn all along the road. Only
when I got back to my company did I find out that the
Confederates in the city of Galveston had held on better
than we had, and they had even won. Their surroundings
helped them because the Northern ships could not unload
their soldiers and had to defend themselves as best they

4. The original text has "Pilliken Spot." A subsequent reference
has also been corrected.

5. Ustyník is making fun of himself by using a pun here. The
Czech word for bag is *pytel*. The word *pytlák*, literally *bagger,* can
mean *numbskull.*

could. The ships were positioned amid their infantry and our artillery so that they had to shoot high in order to avoid harming their own soldiers. Our army was close in and ready to do a lot of damage. Then two of our ships from Houston came with bales of cotton on their decks so that the Northern cannons could not hurt them; in that way they could draw up close and our soldiers could board the ships and force them to surrender. The Northern man-of-war at anchor near Pelican Spit wanted to come to their aid but ran aground on the sand. They didn't think about it for long; they burned their ship and boarded the life-boats, which they took out into the open sea. The ship that had come from New Orleans and that had shot at us got all the way to the harbor but the rest of the ships had already given up. A white flag was hoisted on the ship and the Southerners gave the captain an hour to surrender. An hour later, the steamship turned and left without harm. The Confederate spoils were five ships and two companies of captured soldiers. About 150 on each side were killed or wounded. We thought at that time that the war would end with this "victory."

The next day another ship full of Yankees came from New Orleans, and in order to lure them in we flew the flag of the United States on every ship. The skipper was not familiar with the channel so he sent three of his men to find a harbor pilot. Unfortunately, among the three was a deserter from the Confederacy who hurried off to see his family in Galveston. He was recognized, captured, and eventually shot. His comrades were also captured.

After that, our soldiers were called together, and the colonel asked for two hundred volunteers to capture the Northern ship. I volunteered, and that evening we boarded a boat on which two cannons had been mounted. The steamship pulled us out to sea and left us there. Each one of us had a three-inch-wide piece of cloth attached to us so that we would recognize and not kill each other. We all had to remain below deck. Only the sailors who were dressed in Northern uniforms stayed on deck. It was very dark and calm, and we were forced to remain there until morning. It was only then that we saw at close range an awful ship with big cannons which would perhaps drill our ship full of holes. We raised the flag and gave a sign for the boat to pull up to us. However, the ship did not move, so a captain with two sailors in a lifeboat went over there. But they held the captain and sent the sailors back. We expected our ship to be shot to hell at any moment, but the Northerners most likely were astonished by our presence and simply left. We were greatly relieved when the steamboat came for us and pulled us back to the harbor.

After that, our regiment was moved about three miles from Galveston, and when one of our soldiers, Sam Sweringen, fell ill, he was sent to the hospital in Houston. I had to go too, to take care of him. That was the first time in my life that I had been in a hospital, and I did not close my eyes that night. The patients were wailing, and two of them died. I wanted to leave as soon as it was day, but they wouldn't let me go until eight o'clock. A couple of soldiers there were from our company and they asked me to stay. They said that I would have it better there than with the company. I listened to them and became a nurse. I had little work, good food, and a good bed. After about two months a doctor sent me to the country to buy food for the hospital. I was glad that I would be able to go see my parents. I returned three weeks later, after buying bacon, eggs, and other such things. In a short time I was sent shopping again, and when I was sent a third time, I didn't return.

I always had it in my mind to run away to Mexico, and

when I had gone to see my parents the last time, my seventeen-year-old brother had a load of cotton to haul for the government. That was in the fall of 1863, but we couldn't leave until the spring. I had been at my parents' home for three weeks when a group of soldiers arrived, looking for runaways or for those who didn't want to be drafted. They had scarcely seen me when they asked me if I was a soldier. I said that I was and that I would show them my pass. I had one, but it did not state the date on which I was supposed to return. I had to go with them. Nine miles from my parents' farm we spent the night, and on the next day we went to Bellville. They had caught fifteen of us. At the courthouse I was the first to be brought before the examining officer. He said that he would hold on to my pass and give me what he claimed to be a better one. I would have to report to the hospital within eight days.

I went home with not even the slightest intention of serving any more. I was eager to go to Mexico. I had a friend named Krištof, and I asked if I could stay with him until spring, when I would go with my brother to Mexico. I knew that no one would look for me at Krištof's. His son served in the Southern army in Mississippi, and he himself was too old for the service. The family agreed to take me in, but I left again to spend a few more days with my family. When I returned, I was dressed like a woman because there were no young men to be seen during that time. My sister had to come by herself to take my horse back home. I had it good at Krištof's. Whenever the dog barked, someone from the family would go outside and then give me a signal as to whether or not I had to go and hide. So this is how I spent the winter.

One night in the spring I left for home, where everything for the trip to Mexico had been prepared. We left very early, hauling four bales of cotton covered by canvas.

A place was left for me between the bales. We had enough food for three months: several bushels of cornmeal, one hundred pounds of bacon, thirty dozen eggs, several bushels of sweet potatoes, and two bushels of sweet potatoes that had been cut up and roasted in order to make coffee. We set out at the beginning of April in 1864, and on the first day we got to Ganado, where we spent the night on the prairie. On the second day we had to go just four miles to get to the road which led for three hundred miles to Laredo. For eight days I was in the wagon, and no one but my brother knew about me. Just when we reached the Colorado River at Mustang, I crawled out, and the people accompanying us thought that I must have fallen from heaven. I did not hide anymore.

For several days we stayed near Victoria to let the oxen recuperate a little because they had kept themselves alive only by grazing in the wilderness through which we had just passed. At Victoria more carriers joined us, until there were twenty-four wagons in all. The guard in Victoria inspected passes, and there were several among us who didn't have one. To cross the Guadalupe you had to go on the ferry, and the guard was on the other side, so we went around twenty miles farther and crossed the river there.

There were five or six pairs of oxen to every wagon, and of course we left tracks. We were afraid that we would be discovered, but luckily, that didn't happen. We made it across the river all right, and went to Goliad, then on to Gallinas and Panna Maria,[6] where only the Polish lived, still a long way from Laredo. If someone broke a wheel along the way, the carrier had to play wheelwright himself. In May and June it was awfully hot, the roads were dry, and if you didn't have a good wagon, the wheels dried

6. The original text has "Santa Maria."

up on you and the iron bands fell off. You had to replace
them right there on the prairie, but that was very hard
to do because there was no water to pour on them.

Both we and our animals suffered due to the lack of
water. Once we had gone two and a half days without
water. I found water in a pool about a mile from the
road, but more than three hundred head of dead cattle
lay around the pool—they had gotten down into the mud
but couldn't get out. I looked for a spot where the ground
had not been ruined. It was about five feet wide, and we
decided to water one team at a time. But the oxen, as
soon as they smelled the water, rushed to it, and so it happened that several got stuck. It took us half a day of hard
work to pull those out with the help of the other ones.
The remaining nasty water was all that we had for ourselves. The next day I went to find some better water, and
when I came upon a stream about five miles away, I eagerly
got down to drink. But I was sorely disappointed to find
out that it was salty. I brought this sad news back to camp,
and again set out to find water. This time I was luckier—
I found water about three miles away, and it was good.
We made our camp there and stayed four days. We had
a Mexican with us who knew how to play the violin and
every night there was a party—which we all attended. We
always camped with about five or six wagons in a bunch,
and altogether there were about thirty wagons. I danced,
then, for the first time in my life.

When our animals had rested up, we set out across the
wilderness again, and again we had only a little water for
us to drink and a little for the oxen. There was so little
that we had to unhitch a few of the oxen and let them
go because they had grown so weak. We had to catch wild
oxen to take their places, and that was a lot of hard work.
It was even more work to harness them. In this way we

covered the final one hundred miles. Now my brother and I began to worry about what we were going to do with our oxen and wagon, because we wanted to stay in Mexico. We wanted to sell them, but there was no buyer. However, it happened that we were joined by a certain German who was riding a horse. When he found out that we would sell, he said that he would buy our things, although his wagon was lagging behind. We agreed on $250.00, although it had cost us twice as much. He paid us in Laredo, where we had the cotton unloaded. We had some difficulty there, because we didn't want to unload the cotton until we had received our $225.00 in pay. Finally, one of the buyers who didn't have ready cash gave me two bales of cotton for my pay. I was satisfied with that, and I sold them for $240.00, so that I now had $490.00 in all.

After that we went about two miles out of town, and we settled down there, transferring our animals to their owner. Then we began wondering how we were going to get across the river to Mexico. On our side there was a strong guard, and since I was on the run I knew that I would be imprisoned and shot if I gave myself away. In spite of that, the next day I went to the official who issued passes to Mexico and asked for one. He asked me if I was a soldier, but I denied it and said that I was going to Mexico for some goods that I needed. I got a pass for six days and eagerly approached the river. There the soldier stopped me, but when he saw the pass he allowed me to go. On the ferry I happily got to Mexican soil—free, among coarse people.

On the day after I arrived, the man who had bought our draft animals came over. He borrowed thirty-five dollars from me. I knew that he wasn't going to pay me back, but I gave it to him anyway so as not to betray my brother who was still in Texas and to whom I had sent my pass. He came to Laredo after I did. We remained in Laredo for about fourteen days. Work there was hard to find, and everything was expensive. A barrel of white flour cost forty dollars, and a bushel of corn was seven dollars. A pound of coffee was fifty cents, and one meal in a tavern was a dollar and a half. A Jew allowed us to stay in his yard, and we also took our meals there. We worked at whatever we could find, making about five dollars a day for the two of us. There wasn't much work, however, and after fourteen days, we left for Matamoros, as drivers in the service of a Mexican. I was promised ten dollars if I took the wagon with five pair of oxen and eight bales of cotton to Matamoros, three hundred miles away. That was very little pay but it was an opportunity to get to Matamoros. Four wagons with Mexican drivers had to go with us.

But we had barely loaded up when a Spaniard came and bought the wagon and the Texas oxen. Our pay was lost. I complained to him about my bad luck and he offered the promised sum to my brother and me if we would go with one of the wagons. I accepted, but I wouldn't go with Mexican draft animals in front; I didn't even want to harness them. The yoke drew up on the ox's forehead with a strap and that was all. Three pairs of oxen were hitched to the wagon, which contained six bales of cotton. A cane with an iron spike was placed in my hand. I was supposed to use it to keep the oxen moving. We stopped in front of a business, and the owner of the wagons called us all inside. He bought us food for our long trip—two bushels of corn, one bushel of beans, some coffee, and sugar which was black and came in pieces that looked like loaves. You had to put it into water and heat it over a fire before it would dissolve. He gave us instructions about how we were to behave on the trip, and I asked

for an advance on my pay. He gave me one dollar. We went
through a wilderness of cactus and mesquite, and wherever night overtook us, that's where we made our camp.
I made the fire, and brother fetched some water. One of
the Mexicans put dried meat and corn in the kettle, and
when the corn was cooked, he took it out and let it set
until the hulls of the kernels peeled off. Then he ground
it up on a twelve- by eighteen-inch stone, and from this
flour he made flat cakes and placed them on a baking tin.
These are the Mexican tortillas.[7] At the same time, I
cooked beans, coffee, and beef. I threw the fat cut from
the beef into the beans. And that was our fare for the entire thirty days of our journey. Of course, in the last days,
the meat already had worms in it. The oxen ate cactus
after we had burned off the needles. For beds we had raw
cowhides, with yokes under our heads. At night I always
covered up my money with sand, for robbers came around
every day and asked my companions whether I had any
money. At that time few white men passed through that
country, because they were afraid of being robbed and
killed. When someone was killed, they would stick a little cross in that spot, or more crosses if more than one
had been killed. I myself saw up to four crosses on some
of the trees. In the city of Guerrero I bought some bread
for fifty cents and divided it among the others, and in Co-
margo [sic] I did the same thing, just for myself, and my
companions saw that the dollar I had received from the
owner of the wagons was spent.

Finally, after thirty-two days, we got to Matamoros in
the month of August, 1864. After we unloaded the cotton, I received my nine dollars, and I handed over the animals. As I carefully thought about my money, we went

7. The original text has "tortollas."

to the inn, which was owned by a German. We asked him if we could work for room and board, but he asked right off if we had money to pay for two days. When I agreed and paid, he said that I could get work, and in a short time I went to work at his inn for thirty-five dollars per month, plus board. My brother found work in a cotton gin for two dollars a day. He paid four dollars and fifty cents a week for his board.

Three months later, the German went bankrupt, and then I worked with my brother. During that time, neighbors from Texas often showed up, so I knew how my parents were doing. I bought goods for them and often sent money home. In January of 1865 many groups of Confederates showed up there, so wages fell and crime increased so much that everyone was afraid for his life. In February of that same year several of us agreed to go to St. Louis. Included in the group with me were Josef Ustyník, Frant. Kunc, Vincenc Šiller, Josef Hájek, and two Germans, Jakub Strauss and Jakub Kinkler. On January 15, 1865, we left Matamoros on foot and went to Bagdad, 38 miles away. The next day we crossed over to the Texas side of the river and went 106 miles farther to the island of Brazos Santiago, where the Northern army was encamped. The guard took us to the provost-marshal, who put us under house arrest in a place that was full of insects. After two days we were questioned by the provost-marshal, and urged to join the Northern army. However, they released me because I was on the run from the Confederates, and later they released the others.

We all received a free steamship ticket to New Orleans. It was the old army transport *Thomas E. Sparks*. We got on board and waited for four days until the sea quieted down a little. There were about two hundred people on the ship. The stormy weather did not come the next day, and the captain thought we could sail. Although the marshal tried to talk him out of it, the captain nevertheless did set sail, but before we made it to the open sea we ran aground three times. We thought the end was near. As soon as we laid eyes on the deep blue sea, another misfortune occurred. The engine quit running, and it was a fearful night as we were tossed about by the waves until the engine was fixed. In the morning, the ocean calmed down and we sailed farther, but the engine repeatedly broke down, so that we didn't want to get out into the open sea.

And so we reached Velasco, where there were several men-of-war. One of them approached our ship, and our captain was informed about the enemy. He said that our engine was not working, and then the big ship took us in tow and pulled us into Galveston, where fourteen men-of-war, heavily armed with cannons, were at anchor. It was frightening just to look at them. Our engine was soon fixed and again we sailed out on the open sea. We sailed the whole night, and in the morning we couldn't see anything but water around us. All at once we saw a dark cloud in the northern sky, and the captain immediately turned the ship to the north. A wind sprang up and we let down the anchor as soon as we spotted dry land. The ship was horribly tossed about, and this lasted for a full twenty-four hours. That was already the tenth day of the trip, and since we had been given food for only four days, we suffered from hunger pains.

On that same day the sailors noticed that the ship had had a hole torn in it by the previous storm and that it was filling with water. The captain immediately rushed with his men to the pumps, but they found out that these were not working. There was nothing left to do but bail out the water with buckets and this we all did. It's easy to understand why we didn't like this since we were weak from hunger, so we started to gripe. The ship was saved, but the stoker had to pick the coal out of the water to feed the engine, which had begun to work again, but only sporadically. We finally caught sight of the Louisiana shore, and, two hours later, sailed into the mouth of the Mississippi. We sailed all day, and when night fell, the sailors robbed every one of us of our possessions. They took my brother's hat off his head; from others they took money, from one a trunk and another his boots. I had over $150.00 in a thin belt on my body, but I had a soldier's belt around my clothes, so no one thought I had any money on me.

In the morning we approached New Orleans, and the guard took us to the provost-marshal. After he looked over our passes, he sent us to a guardhouse, where we were given enough food for two days. After that, we were taken to the port, where we were told to buy enough food for eight days. We did so, and also bought some liquor before we boarded the steamship. It was full of Northern soldiers, black and white. In every port some got on and some got off so that we were always surrounded by soldiers that we didn't know. Many of them stole from us. One stole ten dollars from my friend. We told his commanding officer, and he called the soldier up. The soldier didn't want to admit it, so he was taken up to the deck and we were, too. They tied a thin rope to his thumbs and hoisted him up so that only the tips of his toes touched the deck. The soldier spat, and when his mouth was open, the stolen ten-dollar bill was found under his tongue. For the theft the soldier had to remain in the same position for two hours. When the officer finally cut the rope, he fell as if he had been shot, and blood flowed from his nose and mouth. I don't know if he gave up stealing after this punishment.

On the eighth day, at three o'clock in the afternoon,

we reached Cairo, Illinois, and there we boarded a train and went through Illinois to St. Louis. On the train we had the finest of comfort. Each one of us picked out a padded seat, and although a guard locked the door so that none of us could run away, we were all happy to be in the midst of such comfort. The train was scheduled to leave at nine o'clock in the evening, so we had to wait six hours. We were hungry, and I told this to the guard on duty. He said that we would have to call the corporal, and when he came, he said that he would buy some food if we had any money. I gave him two silver dollars, which surprised him. He asked if he could take them and use greenbacks. I agreed. At that time the stores in the North had little gold or silver. Money was very scarce. He brought us our food and gave me back a dollar. But I returned it to him. At nine o'clock the corporal unlocked the door, and the people came aboard. They all had to show their passes of course. They crowded in, but no one sat by us. They would rather stand up than risk getting lice from our coats. A lieutenant sat down by me and we got along well together all the way to St. Louis.

Here we were put up in the Greenbaum Hotel. We changed into a new set of clothes and they burned the old ones in the hotel yard. The next day we went out and tried to find work, but we didn't find any. F. Kunc, one of our countrymen, had an aunt in St. Louis, and he knew the address. We went looking for her and did indeed find her. She didn't want to let us in the house. Only when Kunc introduced himself did she greet us as countrymen. Seeing that we were looking for work, she said that her husband was working in a factory and that he could get us work there. Kunc stayed at his aunt's and we returned to the hotel. We thought that Kunc was lucky, but in the morning he came back and swore that they were all as poor as beggars and that there was no work there. We all got together and went to the port. We heard several young men speaking Czech there and immediately ran over to them and told them that we were looking for work, that we were from Texas — but before we could finish they branded us with the cry "Robbers!" One of them, apparently to show that he knew something about geography, said that Texas was in South America below Mexico and that shortly we would get a whipping rather than work. We left without saying goodbye and went to the hotel and paid our bill. Then we went over to Illinois, where we got on a train and traveled to Belleville.

We set out to find work on a farm and agreed that we would take the first job we were offered. J. Strauss found a job that same day and the next day J. Hájek did, too. But my brother and I and F. Kunc returned to our hotel in St. Louis. The hotel manager told us about a job feeding army horses. It was about two miles out of town, and the pay was twenty dollars a month, plus board. Each of us had to care for sixteen horses — feed, water, and clean them. We stayed there a month until the horses were sold. In the meantime I found out that my brother-in-law Jan Štefek, also on the run from the Confederates, had deserted before Vicksburg in 1863, and was working in Cairo, Illinois. I wrote him to see if he could find work for me, and he wrote back that I should come because he had found work for one person. I went there by steamboat and got work in a brick factory. My brother and the rest found jobs cutting cord wood along the Mississippi River. They bought axes, food, and utensils, and went into the forest, where they were shown to the place to cut the wood. They didn't stay long because the pay was low, and so they went to Cairo.

By that time, the Civil War had ended, and we returned

to our parents in Texas. On June 27, 1865, we arrived in Cat Spring, and the joy of our parents cannot be described, especially that of my mother. A big celebration was planned for the Fourth of July, to commemorate the Union victory. That was the first time I had ever taken part in such a party. I was twenty-three years old, and my brother was twenty-one. There were many Germans and some Czechs at the celebration. Soon after that, mother and my ten-year-old sister got sick. My sister died two days later, and mother passed away two days after my sister. We had been home for barely a month, and now father remained with us two sons and my twenty-five-year-old married sister. I also came down with influenza and suffered with it for three months.

In August, my sister and her husband moved to Nelsonville, and father began to pine for my mother and sister. I cooked for my father, but food had lost its flavor for him. I knew that he would rather have a woman cooking for him, so I told him that I was going away. He agreed with my decision. I took my clothes, which weren't worth much more than five dollars, and my horse and saddle. I had seventy dollars in ready cash. Father wanted the money that I had saved in Mexico, but I didn't give it to him. I rode horseback to my brother-in-law's in Nelsonville. I kept myself busy with cotton and did some carpentry work until Christmas, making about forty dollars. I rented fourteen acres for three dollars an acre and bought a pair of oxen, a plow, some corn, and hay before all my money was gone. I had to pay my brother-in-law fifty dollars a year for board. In the meantime my brother had also left my father and was in the service of Mr. Sušeň in Nelsonville. Now my father called for me.

I went to him, and I was amazed at the way he had changed in the short time since mother had died. His mind was a little unbalanced. He asked me to sell the farm because he couldn't live there anymore. He wanted to live with us. I promised him that I would oblige him. I went around to see a neighbor and offered him the fifty-acre farm for $500.00. Father had some cattle, and the neighbor wanted them added into the bargain. Father agreed, sold the farm, and moved to Nelsonville. That was in January of 1866. Father and I stayed with my brother-in-law that year. Father had sold three bales of cotton in Brenham for $400.00. From that sum he kept $100.00 and gave $100.00 each to me, my brother, and my sister. He pined away the whole year. I paid for my board for the year, bought some clothes, and was penniless once again. Brother got married in January of 1867 and, along with father, bought a farm from the Sušeňs in Nelsonville for $900.00. I worked a field in 1866 and got $180.00 for cotton, $50.00 for corn, and $15.00 for millet, $60.00 for the oxen, and $16.00 for the plow. From that money I paid my rent and other debts, and I had $200.00 left. In 1867 I went to work for Petr Mikeska for fourteen months. My pay was $270.00. In 1868 I worked in carpentry and in the fall at W. Fotrama's gin five miles from Wesley. In 1869 I worked in the gin that Ar. Cole rented near Nelsonville. The job lasted four months and I made $160.00. In 1870, my eye hurt all year, and the doctor's bill and the cost of the medicinal baths was $200.00, but my eye got better. In 1871 I went to work for Mr. J. W. Bethany in Nelsonville. He had a steam gin, saw, and mill, and I had to see that all of it was working properly. For that I got $500.00 a year, as well as my board, laundry, and a room. I did that for two years and six months.

In 1873 I got married, taking for my wife Vincenc Šiller's eighteen-year-old daughter, who had been born in Industry. Her parents were from Čermná in Bohemia, and from there they had immigrated to Moravia, and then to Texas. I rented the mill from Mr. Bethany on halves, and everything went well for us. That year my wife was very homesick, but she recovered and gave me the gift of a son. In 1874 I moved to my father-in-law's place in Industry. Hoping to find some kind of home for my family, I went by train three hundred miles farther on to Cooke County.[8] In Sherman I got off the train to take a look at the countryside. In a shop there I asked the owner if anyone ever came in from the county. He said yes, and pointed to a wagon standing outside. Nobody was in the wagon, but I stood there until the owner came, and I asked him for a ride. He was reluctant, saying that he had a heavy load. I said that I would be going on foot otherwise, but he didn't want to take me and was determined not to. Evening was approaching, and he had to go home, so he jumped on the wagon and urged on his horses, but I was close behind him. As he came down the hill, I jumped on the wagon and rode along. Now, seeing that he wasn't going to get rid of me, he asked me to stay on the wagon. After nightfall, he stopped in a small clump of trees and said that we would spend the night there. I helped him with the horses; then we made a fire and cooked supper. After supper he told me that he hadn't wanted to give me a ride because he thought I was a robber, but that now he was satisfied that I wasn't. He praised the countryside around there, but I didn't like it. The next day we arrived at his place, and many other farmers were waiting for him and the supplies. Coffee was cooked, biscuits were baked, and everyone ate.

8. The original text has "Cook County." Subsequent references have also been corrected. The city of Sherman is actually located in neighboring Grayson County.

When I got up the next day, I asked him how much I owed him, and he said "nothing." I gave him about two dollars and went on foot twelve more miles to Gainesville. There I found out that some countrymen lived twenty-two miles away, so I set out in that direction. When night fell I asked at the first farmhouse I came to about lodging. They said that I should go two miles farther and that I would find a place there. Eagerly I went on my way, walking up to the building, and called out. A person came out, and I asked him about lodging there. He said that I could not stay, but I told him that I couldn't go any farther. Nevertheless, I had to go on. I had already covered thirty miles, the sun had already set, and I was alone in the forest. I walked on for two more miles and came to a farmhouse. Once again I asked for a night's lodging. A young boy tried to send me farther, but I said that I couldn't go any farther, and directed myself to the porch. The boy again warned me to move on, but I was so tired that I couldn't go any farther. I told him that I wasn't going to go even if he tried to kill me. He let me sit, and in a while the owner came out; when he heard that he had a foreigner who didn't want to leave his farm, he asked me what I wanted. I said a night's lodging. He said that his wife had died and that he wouldn't let anybody stay. I simply couldn't go any farther, so I told him that if he would give me a cup of coffee I would pay him for it. He talked with me for about fifteen minutes; then the supper bell rang and the gentleman invited me to go with him. I couldn't get to my feet, so he helped me, and we sat down at the supper table. When I had eaten he gave me a bed, and, in the morning, breakfast. He then offered to let me use that day to rest. I accepted, and the next day he went with me to Dexter, a small town about twelve miles from his farm. I paid him the $2.50 that he requested. In Dexter, I found out that there were some Moravians about eight miles from there, and so I set out on the road. First of all, I came to the farm of a Mr. Bednář. They were in the middle of plowing and were amazed to see a foreigner who knew Moravian.[9] They accepted me cheerfully and treated me royally. That same day I went with Mr. Bednář to the home of his son, who was renting land from Col. J. Bolden. I remained there overnight. In the morning all the Moravians got together, and I acted as their interpreter. This American had helped them as best he could. I stayed at his place for two days and then told him that I was looking for a home for my own family. He offered me the use of a horse in order to take a look at the countryside, and I was happy to accept. The next morning I went to Gainesville, twenty-two miles away. There I spent the night and then went to Montague County.

Toward evening I came up to a building in the forest which was surrounded by posts ten feet high. When I hollered, a man with a big pistol in his belt came out and asked me what I wanted. I said that I wanted a place to spend the night. When I had answered his second question by saying that I was a respectable person, he told me to unsaddle my horse and tie him in the small pasture, and then to follow him up to the porch. In a short while, eight men arrived, all of them with pistols in their belts. I asked the man why he had such a high fence, and he said it was because of the robbers and the Indians. Some of the men started to milk the cows, while some cut wood and others cooked supper. After supper they called the dogs and brought them into the stockade. You should have heard the barking. I was afraid for my horse, but the owner told me not to worry, the dogs could take care of thirty

9. Ustyník means a Moravian dialect of Czech.

Indians and the men themselves could handle one hundred more. From what I had seen of Cooke County so far I didn't like it, and now Montague County was even worse. Today, however, that area is much more suitable for settlement.

I didn't go far into Montague County, but from what I had seen in those two days, I thought there was nothing but lawlessness there. After that I returned to Cooke County, and I really liked the area about four miles northwest of Gainesville. It was well situated and there was good water, so I decided to settle there. At that time it was possible to get an acre of land for $2.50. From there I went into the Indian Territory, which I liked very much, but you couldn't buy any land there unless you married an Indian. I went on about seventy-five miles farther and then returned to Cooke County. I returned the borrowed horse, stayed there a couple of days, and then staked a claim to the aforementioned land between Big Elm and Little Elm.

Then I went back to my wife, who was at the home of her brother-in-law, J. Mašík, in Wesley, Washington County. That was about the first of June, and by the end of July I was already moving to Cooke County, whose county seat is Gainesville. In that town I rented a house and looked for work so that I could at least earn a living. But I didn't find anything. It was terribly dry, and anyone who had water in his well kept it locked up. I stole water from a miller who had to haul it from a stream three miles away. I began to feel homesick in that country, and once when I asked one of the local settlers about rain, he said that sometimes it didn't rain for two years.

There were ranchers in the area who had many cattle and a lot of land, and they didn't let anything stand in their way. When they came to town they threw a lot of money around, and everybody had to take a lot off of them and cater to them, even pretend to like them, because they all wore pistols, and no law officers were around. I also saw buffalo hunters there. They arrived hauling four wagons full of hides and dried meat. With all of this produce they bought supplies—whiskey, powder, lead, flour, sugar, coffee, tobacco. After shooting up the place, they left. Often there were forty or more of them together.

In July and August the prairie completely dried up, and the grass looked like snow lying across the valley. There was no work, and, of course, no credit, so I decided to return to either Austin or Washington County. I bought a horse for $165.00 and traded him for a cook stove and a bed. So I had three horses, a Studebaker wagon covered with canvas, and $95.00. My wife didn't like the idea of a three-hundred-mile trip; she was afraid that robbers would kill us or steal our horses. She was right to be afraid, but the train cost too much, and so I loaded all our belongings on the wagon.

On the first day of September, 1874, my wife, our eleven-month-old son, and I set out on the road. We went through wilderness mostly, through the counties of Cooke, Denton, and Tarrant, and in Fort Worth I bought some food. The country we went through was dry, and we lacked for water, sometimes having to go as far as forty miles to find it. So we passed through Johnson County to Cleburne, and then through Hill County. We met with danger in several places. Several times armed riders came toward us, but they did not harm us because we were ragged and barefoot, and they must have taken us for poor people. However, our attractive team did puzzle them, and I had to watch my horses very closely during the entire trip, sometimes staying up all night. For the most part, the land was slightly hilly prairie with black soil. For eighty miles we followed the cattle trail which the cowboys used to drive their stock to the Indian Territory and Kansas. We could barely make it through some places with our wagon. For the last twenty miles, we went through Tarrant County, where water was scarce, and once when we met two riders, I asked about water. They answered courteously and said that I should travel fifteen miles farther down the cattle trail which ran across the prairie, until I saw a forest. In the forest there was a stream with water, about half a mile to the right of the trail. Just then some Mexicans came up, driving some horses, and I asked them where they were coming from. They said they had come from Kansas, where they had driven cattle for some Texas cattlemen. We looked for the water up ahead, and when we spotted the forest, we were hopeful, and urged the horses on. About half a mile from the creek, the trail turned to the right and at that point we beheld two canvas-covered wagons in front of us, standing at the edge of the creek. We were sure that there must be water there, but when we arrived we found none. I went up to the wagons, but both were empty, and there was not a soul around. Yokes for four or five teams of oxen lay by each wagon, as if they had just been unharnessed. Everything was half grown over with grass, and the animals were nowhere to be seen. I concluded that the owners of the oxen must have been robbed and murdered. Judging from the height of the grass, I would say that it had happened not more than a month earlier. As we sadly traveled along the creek on the right side, the Mexicans I have mentioned rode up. Not finding any water, they unsaddled their horses and let them graze.

We went on, however, and when we had crossed the creek, we went on two miles farther to a hill. To the right we could see a small farm, and on the left side two men were riding across the prairie. We went to the left. I became suspicious when they, seeing that our paths were going to cross, got down from their horses, let them graze, and then remounted at just the right time in order to meet with us. When they began to ride, I stopped. But then they stopped. And when I came farther, they did, too. I didn't like it, but I knew that we would have to meet. One of them stopped in front of us, and the other was on our right side. They had Winchesters and pistols in their leather coats and they looked like highwaymen to us. They asked us where we were moving to. I said to Austin County and told them we had been in Cooke County. I also explained to them that in Cooke County I had been unable to find work and earn a living. They said that I had nice horses and so I must have money. I answered that I had spent all my money on the horses and that I wanted to leave. They said that I shouldn't hurry because they wanted to talk to me some more. I declined, saying that my animals were thirsty and I had to get them to water. I must have said the right thing, because they told me that if I needed anything they would help me, and that if I would go to the farm lying to our right, I would find plenty of water and even some corn. The farm belonged to them and I was welcome to camp there. They said that they were looking for a mule that had wandered off and asked if I had seen it. I told them that behind us, somewhere below the hill, there were twelve Mexicans, and perhaps they knew about the mule. When they heard that, they left without a word and rode away to the farm on the right. I believe that mentioning the Mexicans saved us.[10] We didn't see either one of them after that.

There were small farms on both sides of the trail, and

10. Apparently Ustyník believes that the men left because they were afraid of a confrontation with the Mexicans.

when it grew dark we found water and spent the night. It rained all night long. The next day we didn't get very far because the trail led across the blackland prairie, and the wet soil clung to the wheels. In the evening we camped after dark in a small grove, and in the morning I saw that we had stopped the wagon directly over a grave. It went better for us after that, and in two days we came to a small business at a crossroads, where I asked the way to Towash and whether they had anything for sale.[11] They should have been ashamed of the stuff they sold there. I bought some sardines for twenty-five cents.

We went on for about two miles and came to a stream where there was plenty of water. As it was noon, I unharnessed the horses, watered them, and let them graze. We were getting ready to eat the sardines when four armed men rode up. They quickly got off their horses and said that they would eat with us. I told them that I didn't have anything other than twenty-five cents' worth of sardines and some crackers, but that I would divide that with them. Seeing that I was a poor man they got back on their horses and rode away, to our relief.

It was a very difficult way to travel, but slowly we got closer to home. I had to go through the small town of Towash in Hill County, but it wasn't easy to find off that trail. I had to ask directions of everyone that I met. I had expected to arrive there before sunset, but the sun had already set, and I had no idea where the town was. I was just coming down a hill when two of the wheels were damaged, and the horses could barely hold the wagon up. It bounced from stone to stone, until we found ourselves in a deep creek bed, beyond which stretched a big hill. It

11. The original text has "Tanesh." Subsequent references have also been corrected.

was already dark, and so I got down from the wagon and walked up to the hill. It was steep, the horses were tired, and I had just begun to climb it when a man rode up. He told me that to get to Towash I would have to go back two miles. My wife threw a fit, moaning that she didn't get married in order to go running around foreign lands in the night, among cliffs and mountain tops, but she wasn't suffering any more than I was. Anyway, the experience was good for her. At least she would be able to tell the difference between good and bad in the future. We were fortunate to have good horses, and we made it to the top. I saw a light about half a mile in front of me, and stopped about one hundred feet in front of a building. We stayed there all night and slept well, too.

In the morning I went to the farm to buy corn. The farmer asked me where I was headed, and when he found out that I was going to my old home place, he said that he had a brother, Dr. Williams, in Nelsonville. He told me to count out fifty-five ears; that would be one bushel. I really had something heavy to carry, for the ears were very big and heavy. I asked him how much he wanted for the corn. He said that I didn't owe anything and that if I wanted milk I could have it in about half an hour. When he brought it, he asked me what I intended to do. I said to gin cotton, and he told me that in Towash there was a gin for sale cheap. It was a mile from his farm, and the farmer wanted me to buy it because I could make a lot of money. When I said that I had only a little money, he offered me a loan and said that he would go in with me. I agreed, and he saddled his horse. I didn't have a saddle and had to laugh because I was going into what I thought was a big town in order to buy this gin on an unsaddled horse.

We came to a beautiful valley, and the fields were green

with nice corn and good cotton. Land there cost fifty to sixty dollars an acre. Only three wooden buildings stood in front of us. That was the famous town. There was an old store, but it contained no goods. Several men stood around, whittling wood and chewing tobacco. Mr. Williams introduced me and said that I wanted to buy the gin. The owner of the gin came up and offered to show it to me. It looked as if a big battle had taken place there. Everything was broken and thrown about, with posts rotting in the ground, the circular saw falling apart, the wall around the kettle braced up, the press so cracked that it didn't look like a machine at all, and the engine looking as if a locomotive had destroyed it. We went upstairs where the cotton was ginned, and all the parts were there all right, but they were all broken up, and you had to be careful not to fall down and break a leg when you walked across the floor. The owner talked as if I could buy it all very cheaply. Where something was missing, he explained, I could fix it cheaply and make a lot of money. He added up on paper what everything was worth, and he said it came to three thousand dollars, including the lot. He said I could make that much in a single year but that he would let me have it for fifteen hundred dollars. I saw that it was a bad deal, so I told him that the gin was worthless and left with Mr. Williams. I stayed there that day.

The next day we went on farther. At noon we came to the Brazos River and we crossed it into Bosque County. Then we arrived in the town of Valley Mills, and I wanted to buy corn for the horses. A businessman was asking a dollar per bushel, but I had been paying fifty cents, so I didn't buy any. When we crossed the Bosque River, we entered open country and camped on the prairie. Along the trail there was a large farm and a big field of corn. There I pulled several ears for the horses, although I was really afraid while I was doing it. In the morning it was Sunday, and I went to a farmer to buy some corn, but he said that he would sell no corn on Sunday and would not take any money. But then he thought it over and said that I could pick as much as I needed. I took about a bushel and laid fifty cents on the fence as I left. By the time I was back on my horse he already had the money in his pocket. I guess that wasn't a sin.

That day, we got to Comanche Springs, where there was good spring water. Then we went through parts of McLennan and Coryell counties and arrived in Bell County, in the town of Belton, where I bought some food. From there we went to Salado, and then past Florence to Georgetown, the county seat. Then through the counties of Brazos, Bastrop, and Lee, to Giddings, Ledbetter, Round Top, and Shelby. Finally, we got to my father-in-law's place at Industry, the end of the trip. It had taken us eighteen days to travel that three hundred miles, and we had seen a lot of good as well as bad territory along the way.

In 1889, I bought a five-hundred-acre farm from an old slaveowner named Allen. The buildings and fences were broken. I built six renter's buildings and fences, and I cleared more forest. Every year I added more fields and rented them out. But without a good manager on a farm, it's hard to make a profit. In September of the same year I bought a steam-driven cotton gin, circular saw, and corn mill in Wesley from L. Mašík and J. Šebesta for four thousand dollars. I paid them twelve hundred dollars and borrowed the rest. The first year I had a lot of expenses because everything wasn't in good working order, but since then I've been lucky.

In 1895 I sold them all and moved to a farm which I bought three miles from Wesley. There I have lived up to this time. For the first four years we had good crops, but cotton was cheap, four to five cents a pound. Then came the wet years, and cotton production was low, but the price was ten to eleven cents a pound. Last year we had a good crop. Cotton is our main crop, but anything will grow here if a person devotes enough work to it. As far as storms or hail is concerned, I've lived here for forty-three years and I've never suffered any damage. You couldn't find a better plot of land anywhere. There is plenty of water from springs and wells, plenty of trees, and enough hay, too. I paid twelve dollars an acre, but since I have improved it, it is worth twenty-five dollars an acre to me. If you could get a good manager and have some help you could do quite well.

Seven children were born from our marriage, three boys and four girls. Our oldest son met with an accident when he was young. My wife and her sister Klukanová were preparing a Christmas tree for the children, who were very happy when they were allowed to see it. But a young American boy who had gone into another room put on a mask, ran back, and jumped toward my boy. He was so frightened that he went into an epileptic fit. We immediately took him home, sent for the doctor, and stayed up with him all night. The doctor was afraid that the sickness would pass away only to return as soon as the boy was the least bit frightened. We have suffered a lot over this. He lost the ability to speak; now he speaks poorly, but he can converse with someone who is often with him. I took him to San Antonio and later to St. Louis, but no doctor has helped him. As he grew up, his seizures quit coming. I sent him to school for three years in Austin but that only helped a little. I do what I can for him, and it has cost me a lot of money. He stays at home and he helps where he can, but he can't work with the livestock.

Vilém, the second son, has been in the jewelry business for three years. He is single and twenty-six years old. Jan, the third son, is thirteen. He still lives at home and goes to school. Libuše, the oldest daughter, is married to Anton Hradečný, a Moravian, who is an agent for a New York life insurance company. The second daughter, Alvina, died single at the age of nineteen. The third, Olga, is married to Doctor E. R. Knolle, who comes from a German family but was born in Texas. At home, he speaks English but you can converse with him in Czech, too. He is well liked, has a big practice, and is well-to-do. The fourth, Anna, is nineteen, single, and at home.

I gave them an education, the best I could provide, in English. We don't have Czech schools here. But they know how to read and write Czech.

5 Jan Horák

This essay, which appeared in the *Amerikán národní kalendář* of 1929, is based on the interview of an old Moravian pioneer by L. W. Dongres, whose personal essay appears in the epilogue. Writing in the late twenties, Dongres could already feel nostalgia for the old Czech-Moravian culture that had still been common in Texas around the turn of the century. He provides a frame of reference for Horák's self-history, which is given as a single extended quotation. Dongres's closing statement about Horák, who died before his autobiography could be published, might serve as a motto not only for Dongres's work but also for the present volume: "May his memory live forever."

Horák's Civil War reminiscences dominate this short account. His summary description of a peaceful life after the war as the head of a Czech farming family could, with a few changes, be applied to many like him.

Not far from the old Czech community of Fayetteville, Texas, I found an old Czech settler, Mr. Horák, who had come to America in 1856. Recognizing his mental alertness and his excellent memory, in spite of his eighty-five years, I was reminded of Mr. Geringer.[1] We were both sorry that the old customs of Texas countrymen had passed away. For example, the custom of calling out "Vítám vás!"[2] when approaching the entrance of another's house; and hosts, after thanking you for your visit, would say, "Well, let's have one for the road." The times are gone when the community was so Moravian that one almost couldn't converse in any other language. When I got off the train in 1894, I myself was amazed when a black porter approached me and said, verbatim, in our mother tongue, "Give me your satchel and I'll carry it to the hotel."[3] My colleague Jos. Tápal, the editor of Věstník,[4] took me to the Horák farm. When we had sat down in the "gallery," "Uncle" Horák, after some idle talk about his weak memory, began to relate his story:

I WAS BORN IN 1842 IN HOLIČÍN U HOLEŠOVA in blessed Haná, the heart of dear, sweet Moravia. My father, František Horák, a farmer, had seven children. Of these, my brother Victor in Ammansville and my sister Carolyn Nietche in La Grange are still alive. We set out for America in December of 1855 from Bremen. After eleven weeks, our shabby sailboat landed in Galveston. My father knew old Mr. Reimershoffer in

1. Dongres is probably referring to August Geringer, the publisher of *Amerikán národní kalendář*. (See our introduction.)

2. This phrase literally means "I welcome you." Here it might be translated as "Greetings!"

3. See Dongres's own memoir for another reference to this incident.

4. This Czech-American journal began publication in Fayetteville, Texas in 1912 and is still being published in West, Texas today. It is the official organ of the popular Czech fraternal organization SPJST.

Cat Spring, who was also from Holešov. ([Dongres's] Note: His daughter Clara Reimershofferová died just this year in Galveston. Today the descendants of that forty-eight-year-old patriot speak only German and English. Clara was the last of the family with whom one could converse in our mother tongue.)[5] At that time Cat Spring was still sparsely populated. Only a couple of Germans were there. Father bought a piece of land, and we farmed for two years. Reimershoffer had a store in Cat Spring. Our car, buggy, carriage, etc. consisted of only a pair of oxen with which we went everywhere, even to church. The cotton was hauled to Houston and sold for seven cents a pound. A certain Kinkler had a gin, powered by a team of oxen. At that time Opočenský was there.[6] The Catholic countrymen went to Frelsburg and then to Ross Prairie, where there were also some Moravians. There was no public school. The priests preached and taught in Czech. In spite of the oxen they had to use for transportation and their bare feet, the young people had a great time going to dances.

I was nineteen when the Civil War broke out. My sympathies were with the North. We hated slavery. We came to America so that we could be free, and we wanted everybody to have freedom. At first they took only volunteers, but then they drafted us, using force. There was a lot of informing against one another and general lawlessness. When my time came, I saw that I couldn't run away, so I went along. At first we trained at a camp near Austin, and then they sent us to Brownsville on the Mexican bor-

5. For other references to the Reymershoffers, as the name is usually spelled, see the Lešikar, Ustyník, and Branecký accounts.

6. Rev. Josef Opočenský was the first Czech Protestant minister to organize a church unit in Texas (at Wesley, in Washington County).

Jan Horák.
Photograph reproduced from
the *Amerikán národní kalendář* for 1929.

der. After three weeks, I was able to flee across the Rio Grande River. Not long after that Fr. Bezecný and Jan Petr made it across, too. When there were twenty-five of us, they took us by boat to New Orleans, where they registered us for the Northern army. Petr and I had no stomach for the military, so we looked for some kind of work, but in vain. Hunger forced us into blue coats. They put me in the cavalry, where they had organized a regiment of runaway Texans. We trained there for two weeks, and then they sent us to catch "bushwackers" near Camp Moore. These people were the hard-core Southern slaveowners who made war on their own. They crawled around in the underbrush and shot people from hiding places. They were common murderers. You couldn't run the risk of getting very far from camp. All around were the scattered graves of the victims of these murderers. ([Dongres's] Note: When I lived in the Ozark Mountains, near Springfield, Missouri, I saw many such graves of unfortunate people, the victims of this brother-killing war and of the slaveowners' fanaticism.) Finally, we caught twenty-five of them, and they got the just reward of murderers. I was in the army for two and a half years, but I fought in only one battle. The Southerners were approaching Franklin, near New Orleans. I was in the vanguard. The Southerners began to advance cautiously. A German led us, and he was raging, "Get those slaveowning dogs!" We had six wounded and had lost fourteen horses by the time the slaveowners ran out of the range of our guns.

After the signing of the peace treaty, they sent us to San Antonio, and I was discharged there on October 30, 1865. During the war it was bad at home, and after the war it was even worse. Confederate money—in Baton Rouge, Louisiana, we filled up a basket with it. Our family lived in Ross Prairie. I stayed on the farm for four years and helped. I sort of wanted to get married. It's not good for a person to be alone in this world, and God did not want to take a rib from my body. So in 1870, when I went to work for Jos. Laštovica, I gave up and married Miss Apolena Zapalačová, the daughter of Jan Zapalač from Hrozenkov, who had come to America in 1855. We rented a place from the Zapalačes near Oak Hill. We were there until 1918. The first organization was evangelical and came in 1874.[7] Then a Catholic priest and some sisters came, and now English must be taught, as required by law.

We had five daughters, who are married and live in Columbus, West, Crosby, Needville, and Garwood. We took in an orphan from the orphanage and adopted him. In 1918 we bought a piece of land near Fayetteville, and since then, we have farmed here. Otherwise, our life has gone just like any other. We have our family concerns. What more can I say? It's light during the day and dark at night. It's cold in the winter and hot in the summer. People are always talking a lot of nonsense. I can't complain about anything, and anyway, it wouldn't do any good. I'm waiting peacefully until my hour comes, when I'll be taken away to eternity, where I came from.

[Dongres's] Postscript: Shortly after this autobiography was written for the *Amerikán národní kalendář*, the end for which Uncle Horák had waited so courageously, with a settled peace of mind, really came. May his memory live forever.

7. Horák apparently means the first Czech fraternal organization.

6 *Josef Lebeda*

Although the majority of Texas Czech farmers were almost directly transplanted from their Bohemian and Moravian villages to rural Texas, there were exceptions. As a young man, Josef Lebeda was recruited as a mercenary for Maximilian's army in Mexico and led a life that would be considered exciting by any standards, yet he relates his exotic adventures in a matter-of-fact style. Lebeda found his way to the Czech farming community in Fayette County almost by accident. This short account of his life was published in the *Amerikán národní kalendář* of 1880.

I AM A NATIVE OF ČESKÝ DOBŘÍŠ, IN THE district of Prague, and my name is Josef Lebeda. When they started to recruit soldiers in Bohemia for Maximilian in Mexico, they told us that every volunteer would receive twenty-five gold pieces, and after six years' service, would receive nine acres of land. I enlisted, and when we took our oath, we promised loyalty to the Mexican emperor, come what may.

After the ceremony, I was sent to Lubin for training in the use of weapons. I was there for five full months. The majority of the soldiers concentrated here were Austrians. There were about seven thousand of us, and they divided us into light cavalry and artillery. I became a cavalryman.

At the beginning of December, we went to Terst, and then embarked on four ships on the 15th of December [1865]. By the 29th of January, we were in Vera Cruz. Here we received uniforms and arms. Every man got sixty cartridges, and the bayonets and sabers were sharpened. Four days later, we were put in the field, and by the seventh day, we were in battle. We won, happily, and were moved to the capital city of Mexico, where Maximilian lived. We camped outside the city, and on the second day, the emperor and empress came to greet us. Three musical groups came with them — one Czech, one French, and one Belgian. After he reviewed us, he stood in front of us and announced that he was satisfied with us, that we were good soldiers, and that in time he would reward us.

We stayed here a full month, and then we pursued marauders into the forests, where we remained a month, but without results, for we caught only two old women and two French deserters. Having returned to Mexico City, we stayed there seven months, inactive. Then we were sent to Orizaba for some imprisoned rebel officers, whom we took to Pueblo. A few days later, we saw all of these officers freed, and we heard that they had bought their way out of it, after they promised that they would never again fight against the emperor. Anyway, they returned to the rebel forces, where they paid back their ransom money and rejoined them to fight new battles. Afterward, in May of 1865, we accompanied the empress to Vera Cruz, where she boarded a ship bound for Europe. A second boat was waiting for our Second and Fourth companies and a battery as well. Lieutenant Koudelič went with us. On the third day, we reached the port of Bagdad, and then we went to Matamoros where we stayed two full months. Then, when Bagdad was attacked and pillaged by the rebels, we had to march there by night. Here a skirmish broke out, and we saw that we would have to deal with the blacks, whom we overcame and drove back into the Rio Grande, where almost all of them drowned. Then we didn't have anything to do again, so we went to Matamoros and stayed there seven months. Then, on the 7th of June, 1866, we went with some frieght wagons to Monterrey. We numbered over three thousand men.

The first day went well, but, after that, there were small skirmishes, day after day. We suffered from the lack of water so badly that we lost six to eight men every day. On the 16th of June, at about four o'clock in the morning, we encountered the rebels under General Oiberi; the bloody battle lasted two full hours, and we were defeated. Many corpses from both sides lay on the battlefield, but we couldn't even bury them, because the survivors were captured, made to strip down to their underwear, and imprisoned in a cattle pen in the town of Camargo. Here General Escobedo explained that we should behave well and wait for our liberation. They then brought us water, and so we grew stronger. Three days later, we were moved farther.

They gave us one biscuit a day, and when they had moved us to a small town, they placed us in a cattle pen. Each day we received about a pound of meat, but no salt for it, and no water or bread. We cooked the meat over a fire, without the use of cooking ware. So we remained there in adversity for forty-five days, until they drove us to Monterrey. It was bad for us, as we were barefooted, emaciated, and weak. In Monterrey, they greeted us with music and led us down all the streets of the city, with the church bells ringing. After this they imprisoned us and made us sweep the streets like convicts for four weeks. We made cartridges, too, and when the city no longer

wanted to maintain us, they farmed us out to other surrounding cities. I was sent with thirty others to Dimaris,
forty miles from Monterrey, where they put us to work
in a sugar factory and paid us fifty cents a day, without
board. Our captivity lasted eight months. Then a Mexican lieutenant came with a German and registered the
names of those who wanted to be set free and those who
wanted to return. Of 150 of us, 3 went back and the rest
asked for freedom. We got letters of safe conduct and were
released, but didn't get any money for the road. I went
to Monterrey, where I hired on as a coachman, for six
dollars a month. But I later went to Texas with a few
friends. That was in April, 1867. Our trip to Austin, Texas,
lasted forty-five days. There I got a job with an American
who hauled goods for the army. I was paid ten dollars a
month. While here, I started asking around about other
Czechs in Texas. I found out from a German that many
lived in Fayette County. Happily I found them and was
hired immediately by Mr. Novák for ten dollars a month.
Soon after that, however, I fell ill and was released from
work. When I got well, I found out that there was not
much of a future here for a single lad. So I got married
and obtained my own place, where I remain to this day
among my countrymen, considering myself satisfied and
happy.

7 *Josef and Terezie Jirásek*

This essay appeared in the *Amerikán národní kalendář* of 1929, along with the Jan Horák memoir, and is also based on an interview by L. W. Dongres. Dongres's technique is similar here; most of the text consists of extended, direct quotations from the pioneer farming couple, Mr. and Mrs. Jirásek, and thus it is largely "autobiographical."

The pattern of Czech settlements in Texas after the Civil War can be directly related to the search for new farmland at a reasonable price, and the Jiráseks are not unusual in their several moves.

The New Tabor (Nový Tábor) community in Burleson County, where the Jiráseks farmed for four years, provides one of the most interesting Czech place-names in Texas. The city of Tábor in Bohemia was founded by the Hussites in the fifteenth century and served as their fortress-capital.

They are hardheaded, those who have been brought up in the strict Protestantism which has been preserved through all kinds of persecution in the Czech Krkonoše region, the region Jirásek wrote about in his *Skaláci*.[1]

---

1. Alois Jirásek (1851–1930) was a Czech historical novelist whose works are still read today.

If you were to go to Taylor, Texas, you would find two such hard, though gray, heads living in a beautiful house overgrown by plants.

By chance the Jiráseks are namesakes of the famous novelist.

Mr. Josef Jirásek was born in 1848 in Čermi, Chrudim County (near Landškroun). His father was Josef and his mother was Rosalie, née Barcalová. The parents were strict Protestants of the Helvetic Confession.

M Y FIRST TEACHER WAS A. UHERKA. My first preacher, who taught me the Bible, was Rev. Juren, the father of the Rev. Juren who is buried in Ross Prairie cemetery near Fayetteville. As a child of poor parents, I could not go to school much but had to find work at an early age. During the Austro-Prussian War there was much poverty in that poor region. The main source of income was from weaving and, in the winter, gathering wood.

On October 28, 1867, we set out for America: father, mother, I, brother Ignác (now dead),[2] Frank (now in Cook[e] County, Texas) and sister Rosalie (who later married Jos. Schiler but is now dead), Terezie (now married to Kar. Esteřák, living in Victoria, Texas). Of those who went with us I remember these families: Fr. Rippel, Vinc. Marek, Uncle Vinc. Barcal, Karel Mottl, Jos. Marčák, Jos. Marek.

Seventy souls went in all, all Evangelicals,[3] except one, Jos. Bárta, a Catholic. The sailing ship was named *Texas*. We went through many severe storms. Once they even had

2. This, like all the parenthetical notes, is included in the original text.

3. In Czech writing of this time, the term *Evangelical* is almost synonymous with *Protestant*.

Josef and Terezie Jirásek
and two of their grandchildren.
Photograph reproduced from
the *Amerikán národní kalendář* for 1929.

to board us up. We arrived in Galveston, and from there we went down the bayou by ferry to Houston. Then by rail to Ellinger,[4] sitting on the freight cars that carry lumber. In Ellinger, wagons were waiting for us, and they took us to New Ulm. My father's sister, Mrs. Terezie Schiller, a widow, had lived there for fourteen years and was farming with her two sons. We immediately started picking cotton. We rented a place for five years and worked hard to deserve the American freedom which we had so yearned for in that rotten Austria. Freedom does not grow on trees but springs from the blood of the nation's liberators and from the callouses of its poor people.

Aunt Schiller had paid our way over. When we arrived father owed her $450.00. During the first year, we added another $50.00 to the debt. We had two bales of cotton left for us, and it was impossible to live on that. We moved to Industry, where we rented another farm, and lived there for five years before father bought a farm in Nelsonville.

Nelsonville was a good Evangelical community, both American and Czech. Luck smiled on me there. I was married on January 7, 1872, to Terezie Ježková, my first and last wife, who is now sitting beside me and helping me remember those old times. ([Dongres's] Note: Now let's speak with Mrs. Jirásek.)[5]

I was born in 1855 in Industry, Texas. My mother and father were Anna and Josef Mareš, who had emigrated from Čermi. They came to America with the teacher Mašík in 1854. I was born the year before they moved. All the

4. "Ellington" is the name of the town given in the text, but apparently Ellinger was meant.

5. As Dongres's note indicates, Mrs. Jirásek begins to speak at this point, but the Jiráseks apparently give a combined account later in the text. Dongres's punctuation and organization do not make this clear.

members of our family died in America. Only my sister Rosalie Mačáková in Caldwell is alive. Mother told me that after the trip to America she worked for twenty-five cents a day. That was at Ellertown, on the prairie. Our family bought a piece of land there, about one hundred acres, at twenty-five cents an acre. We were there for twelve years. I was twelve years old when we moved to Veselý.[6]

An Evangelical church was already there, and the pastor was Rev. J. Opočenský. There was also a Czech school. The teacher was Jos. Mašík (who had taught my mother in Europe). The pastors were rotated there: Schiller, who died there; Juren; Chlumský; and Lacjak, who was accidentally shot on a hunting trip. (See *Památník českých evangelických církví v sev. Americe,* Nákladem Křest'anského posla, Chicago, Ill.)

Finally, Fr. B. Zdrůbek took the church. He had a grand reception. Bridesmaids and groomsmen, all of us met him three miles out. Mr. Zdrůbek married us on January 7, 1872. Then we started to farm together.

We lived with my parents on the farm for one year. For a year after that we rented a place. For six years we were in Nelsonville, where our Josef was born. Now he is fifty-three years old and owns his own farm near Taylor, but he lives in town. His wife was born Emilie Lešikarová. They had eleven children, nine of which are still alive, seven of them already on their own. Altogether, he has twenty grandchildren.

For four years we farmed in the community of Nový Tábor, near Caldwell, on a place we rented. Hynek and Frank were born there. Hynek is now in Taylor, where he is a carpenter (three children, three grandchildren). His

---

6. The name of this Czech community in Washington County means *merry* or *cheerful. Veselý* was later anglicized to *Wesley.*

wife was born Frances Tomanová; she died three years ago. Frank is near Waxahatchie, the county seat of Ellis County, where he owns a mattress factory. His first wife was Frances Lešikarová from Seaton, and the second was Ter. Ozimová from Caldwell. They have no living children.

My parents were constantly after us to return to Nelsonville, and so we moved back there. Our daughter Terezie was born there; she has married Josef Lešikar in Taylor. After six years we moved to Rice's Crossing, where, after five years, we bought a farm. Two years later we sold it and bought one near Taylor, where we farmed for eleven years, sold out, and went to Bell County. After staying in Nová Osada[7] for three years, we sold our farm and moved to Baylor County,[8] where we bought a farm near Seymour. We did very well there. They call it the dry west, but I prospered there. I owned four farms. As a result of the strain, I grew sick and sold it all off, which I regret. The only things we didn't have were canary tongues and bird's milk, but everything else we found in abundance, and to this day I'm sorry we left. After seven years, we sold out and after continuous urging from the children, we moved to Taylor to retire. We have been here for ten years. On the 7th of January, 1922, we celebrated our golden wedding anniversary, during which sugar was served in the sugar jar which the bride had received as a wedding gift fifty years before. Old Mr. Mikeska, who is now dead, was at the celebration. He was the father of Dr. Mikeska (whose autobiography has been published in the *kalendář*). Overall, we have twenty-four great-grandchildren, of which the eldest is eighteen years old, and,

7. The name of this community in Bell County can be translated as *new community*.
8. Baylor County is cited in the text as "Bay" County.

as her figure shows, we will become great-great-grandfather and great-great-grandmother.

Mr. Jirásek is a vigorous man, full of fun. He picked a bouquet of roses and said, "If one of us should die, I'll go over to my sister in Smithville and cheer her up with this bouquet. But before that I'll go to Kolovec u Klatov and shoot the bull with the young folks.[9] It's fun to stay with them: I'll take a rest cure with them after returning from the hospital, and we'll never stop laughing." Well, Skaláks. Hard, Helvetic heads, strong in the bad times and full of good humor in the good times.[10]

If only our whole nation could be made up of such qualities so that we could overcome the malice of the world. Their children and grandchildren all know Czech (even now in the third generation), forty-nine sons and daughters of the Hussite nation.

9. Jirásek's reference is unclear. Perhaps the original text was corrupt here.

10. Dongres means *Helvetic* in the religious sense associated with the Helvetic Confession, that is, *Calvinist*.

8 Josef Blažek

Josef Blažek's short memoir, published in the 1906
issue of *Amerikán národní kalendář*, provides yet another example of anticlericalism and suggests the importance of Czech-American fraternal clubs and societies in Texas.

I WAS BORN ON FEBRUARY 16, 1864, IN
Zbejšov u Rosic, Moravia, to a worker's family. Even
as a child I loved to read, but I had to be content
with the catechism, religious tracts, and school readers.
Thanks to our teacher Antonín Trnka, I got to read a great
deal about geography, history, and other academic subjects, because he placed a heavy emphasis on these areas
so that the students from his school would have the best
possible educational background. Even while I was in
school, I had a great distaste for and mistrust of the priesthood, which became even worse when I recognized how
our catechism teacher Hrubeš was deceiving us. In preparation for our first communion he bullied us so about God
that I got a headache. He frightened us by saying that if
someone concealed some kind of sin or if he were to bite
into the communion host, that immediately blood would
run from his nose and ears and that such a sinner would
turn black. He gave us that as an example. Before com-

Josef Blažek.
Photograph reproduced from
the *Amerikán národní kalendář* for 1906.

munion I forgot all that and licked the cream off some goat's milk, and then fear welled up inside me.[1] I'll never forget the trip to the church and the fear that I was going to turn black and all that other stuff, because I hadn't gone to the church to confess that additional sin. I decided not to because I had heard that the priest had really scolded some others for doing that. But I swallowed the host and nothing happened to me, after all, even though I had, in my eagerness, bitten into it. That awakened a suspicion in me, especially when I saw the priest himself, during mass, bite down on his wafer. — Shortly after that a book about the Spanish Inquisition fell into my hands, and that really shook my faith. In my fourteenth year, I was placed as an apprentice to a locksmith in the Zastávka section of town, where there were only miners and tradesmen who did not set great store in God either, and I stayed there two years.

In 1880, I came to Texas with my parents, my two brothers Frank and Jindřich, and my sisters Josefína and Marie, and we settled in Brazos County, near College.[2] In 1882, I was ready to join a group that wanted to organize a local chapter of the ČSPS. However, for reasons not known to me, the group disbanded and its members later founded the Česko-slovanský hospodářský spolek. Countryman Ed. Král taught several of us boys to play brass instruments, and we became known far and wide as excellent musicians. Several times we played at the nearby Agricultural and Mechanical College for end-of-year student celebrations, and the governor of the State of Texas himself praised us. In 1885, my parents and I moved to Butler

---

1. Blažek was afraid because he had broken the required fast on the morning before communion.
2. Blažek refers to College Station as College throughout.

County, Nebraska, but by the fall of the same year, we were back in Texas again. That year I first saw a copy of *Amerikán,* which has helped in my development, especially when, a year later, I began to read *Duch času* and, in it, *Svatá bible pro zasmání.*[3] A completely new and happy life started for me then. Also, I studied typesetting at the newspaper *Slovan* in La Grange, and I met J. E. Kroupa and Hugo Chotek there. When they organized the Farmers' Alliance here in College, I joined. But it was soon disbanded. —In the Česko-slovanský hospodářský spolek, I was elected to the by-laws committee, which runs the organization. I have been the secretary of this organization several times and have conducted funeral services for brothers.[4] In 1866 I married Josefína Marek, and God has blessed us with three daughters and three sons, so that more atheists were brought into the world.

When A. Hradečný took over as editor of *Slovan,* after Jos. Buňata left, he established the Karel Havlíček Borovský Reading Society in Bryan. I was a member and our society organized a Czech school in College. A. Hradečný was chosen as the teacher and I as assistant. The school did not last long, however. Hradečný had to make a six-mile walk to College, which he got tired of doing every Sunday, and there weren't enough dedicated young people. Mr. Josef Buňata, when he was editor of *Slovan,* had tried to establish a ČSPS lodge, and shortly after his departure in 1889, we succeeded. The "Southern Star," ČSPS lodge #158, was founded. I am a charter member and hold some type of office every year.

3. *Duch času* (Spirit of the Times) was a Czech weekly newspaper published in Chicago. *Svatá bible pro zasmání* (The Comic Bible) was a work by F. B. Zdrůbek.
4. Blažek is referring to fellow members of the organization.

In 1893 I bought more land, near what is today the community of Smetana, and two years later, I joined the "Plow and Book" society, for which I helped write the by-laws. I have been secretary for two terms and chairman once. Having met with unfriendly sentiments from some of the members, mostly dyed-in-the-wool Catholics, I quit two years ago and now belong to only the "Southern Star" lodge and the "Jan Žižka" lodge of the Freethinker Society. I seldom take part in political activities.

9 Josef Buňata

Josef Buňata's story illustrates the itinerant life of the
typical Czech-American journalist in the nineteenth and
early twentieth centuries. The fascinating early history
of Czech journals and their editors in the United States
was well chronicled by Tomáš Čapek in his *Padesát let
českého tisku v Americe* (Fifty Years of Czech Press in
America) (1911). Although, as the example of Buňata
shows, Czech journalism in Texas had ties to that in
other sections of the country, particularly the Midwest,
it developed a progressively stronger regional identity
after the first Czech-language newspaper in Texas appeared in La Grange in February, 1879. The publisher
of the weekly *Texan* was František J. Glueckmann, and
the editor was L. L. Hausild.

The *Texan* survived only until July, 1880, when it
was bought by František Lidiak and renamed *Slovan*
(The Slav). Lidiak published the paper until 1885, when
it was purchased by Josef S. Čada, who, as Buňata takes
up the story, sold out to Edward A. Krall (Král). The
source of the enmity between Čada and rival editor Antonín Haidušek, referred to by Buňata, is interesting.
Haidušek was an assimilationist, in favor of English-
language instruction in Czech-American schools, and
Čada was opposed to his views. According to Jan Habe-

nicht, in his *Dějiny Čechův amerických* (History of Czech-Americans) (St. Louis: Hlas, 1904–10), Haidušek saw his chance to discredit Čada when a *Slovan* article praised Czech women and, in the process, compared them to (Anglo) American women, who were said to be so lazy that they would in fact go hungry or, in extreme cases, turn to a life of sin, rather than work. Haidušek translated the article and made it available to the local English-language press. Needless to say, the translated article led to an uproar in the Anglo-American community. An angry mob demanded that Čada leave town within three days. Aided by sympathetic Czechs, Čada defied the ultimatum but, due to the scandal caused by this incident, he soon moved his press to Bryan.

Buňata's most significant contribution to Texas Czech culture was his edition of *Památník Čechoslováků* (The Czechoslovakian memorial volume) in 1920. His memoir was published in the 1936 edition of the *Amerikán národní kalendář*.

IN 1887 I WAS VEGETATING IN BOSTON AFter being fired from my job as a cigar maker. I had reached Boston after suffering the misfortunes of a Czech-American journalist, having quit as editor of *Dělník Americký*. It had gone well for us in Boston, but a strike broke out, and we lost. As a member of the strike committee, I was not only fired, but my name was also put on a blacklist, and so I had no hope of finding a job in the line of work that had supported me and my family when I was not working as a journalist.

During that period of enforced idleness I read a great deal. I went to the Boston Public Library nearly every day. Also, I read Czech newspapers sent to me from my former

Josef Buňata.
Photograph reproduced from
the *Amerikán národní kalendář* for 1936.

workplace in New York, and I corresponded with them, as well. From them I found out that *Slovan,* the first Texas Czech newspaper, was looking for an editor.[1] *Slovan* had been established by several local countrymen in La Grange and later had become the property of countryman J. S. Čada. A. Haidušek, who had gained an excellent reputation among Texas Czechs but did not get along well with Čada, had formed a new periodical, *Svoboda.* Čada had lost face in La Grange and then had moved *Slovan* to Bryan, Texas, but soon thereafter he sold it to E. A. Král. He, in turn, had got hold of a new owner, who had then passed on the ownership of the business. There were now about five owners and each had put about fifty dollars into the business; only countryman Šťastný had as much as three hundred dollars in it, and that was in the form of a promissory note. The printing press was being paid for in installments. A huge debt was attached to that piece of machinery, and everything else was practically worthless.

I had applied for a job as editor of the newspaper, and, of course, the owners gladly hired me. František Škarda had been in Texas at one time to advertise and to pick up subscribers for *Dělnické Listy,* so I was known there as its editor. But the question remained: how to get from Boston to Bryan, Texas? The owners of *Slovan* could barely pay for their newsprint, and I had been reduced to poverty. My wife was making fifteen dollars or more a week as a good cigar maker, and my son, after recovering from an injury to his fingers in the cigar factory, had found work

1. The first Czech-language newspaper in Texas was in fact the *Texan,* which appeared in La Grange in February, 1879. The publisher was František J. Glueckmann, and the editor was L. L. Hausild. The *Texan* survived only until July, 1890, when it was bought by František Lidiak and renamed *Slovan* (Slav). The *Slovan* was published by Lidiak until 1885, when it was purchased by Čada.

in a print shop at five dollars a week. So, as far as our daily needs were concerned, we were okay, but where could we get the money for such a long trip?

Probably the only one of the *Slovan* owners living today is Šťastný. (This was written in 1929.)[2] He already had three hundred dollars in the business, so he couldn't be expected to send me the money for the trip, and the rest of the owners were still worse off. I decided that I would help myself. I asked the publishers of *Slovan* to send me confirmation that I was a legitimate agent of the periodical *Slovan*.

After having been in Boston for about a year and a half, I had made the acquaintance of almost every countryman there. I went to several of them and offered them subscriptions. I think I got about twelve of them to subscribe, and some gave me the full subscription fee for a whole year, which came to three dollars, while others gave me a half-year subscription, or about one dollar. So I had scraped together enough for the trip, and I set out in 1888, shortly after New Year's Day. I made a detour to Bridgeport, where there was a čsps lodge and where I got several more subscribers, and then to New York.[3] New York was like home to me. I stayed there a week and got more than enough subscribers and subscriptions. I went over to Baltimore, from there to Pittsburgh, then to Cleveland, to St. Louis, and from there to Bryan, Texas.

As the former editor of *Dělnické Listy,* I had plenty of acquaintances everywhere. The result of that long trip was

2. This parenthetical comment by the editor appeared in the original text.

3. The Česko-slovanský podporující spolek (ČSPS) was one of the earliest fraternal orders in the United States, beginning informal operations in a St. Louis tavern in 1854.

that I had brought something over three hundred new sub-scribers to *Slovan* and, after paying all the costs of my trip, had a little over ten dollars in my pocket. I was offered a salary of fifty dollars a week. Since almost the whole month I had been on the road was paid for, I entered the editorship without debt and with several dollars in my pocket. The typesetters were Kroupa, who had been employed by *Dělnické Listy* in New York, and Ant. Hradečný, the former publisher of *Lampička* in Chicago.

But *Slovan* was in sad shape. Debts were as plentiful as flowers in the field. There were enough subscribers, something over one thousand, and if they had all paid regularly, the newspaper would have done well, because *Svoboda* at that time was not very popular. Haidušek was the principal owner of the newspaper, but he was a county judge, too, and he didn't have enough time left for his paper.

The printing press at *Slovan* was one month behind in payments, we had to pay rent on our building, and there was also a debt owed to the company we bought paper from. Now they were sending it COD. It was hard to scrape together any money. All the employees were in debt. Up to that time I had been there alone, without my family. I lived with one of the owners, to whom I did not have to pay rent. The typesetters also lived on credit with some of the owners.

When my family came, it was really bad. The children were used to paying for everything with cash, but now we had to buy everything on credit.

They took to picking cotton, and that brought some relief. I set out on the road. I was often invited to various celebrations as a speaker, and during these events I got subscriptions to the paper, and sometimes even got paid myself. I always brought back a reasonable sum of money, but the creditors were always waiting for it, and there was not always enough left for my salary.

I tried to get Šťastný to assume the financial end of the business. As the owner of the promissory note, he could have easily done it; if he had borrowed five hundred dollars, he could have become the sole owner. I figured that the newspaper could have been profitable, considering the number of subscriptions and advertisements. He didn't do it, and, years later, admitted he had lost not only the three hundred but several more, in *Slovan.*

The businessmen who had been giving us goods on credit made Šťastný responsible for the debt, holding him to be the owner. They also brought a so-called judgment against him. According to the law on homesteads, they could not take his farm or draft animals, nor anything necessary for farming, but bales of cotton, yes, and surplus livestock, too. So countryman Šťastný settled with them in order to avoid any more court battles.

Frant. Škarda, after the loss of *Dělnické Listy* in New York, came to Texas and set up a cigar factory in La Grange. He did well in that business; he couldn't find enough workers, though, and so he gladly accepted my offer to work with him again. I gave my notice to leave the paper, moved to La Grange, and became a cigar maker once again.

In place of the weekly *Slovan,* Čada began to publish in Bryan a small monthly entitled *Rolník.* It was only a kind of supplement, and nothing much came of it. At one time, some German carpenters in New York had founded a mutual insurance organization to which I had belonged and whose by-laws I still had. These I translated and published in *Rolník,* and I wrote several articles in which I explained the merits of such an organization. Several local lodges had already been organized by that time, and the Rolnický Vzájemně Ochranný Spolek later grew out of them.[4] It accepted only farmers as members, but, later, countrymen in towns formed a special organization on the same basis.

After I left *Slovan*, Ant. Hradečný accepted the editorship, but that didn't last long, for the printing shop was seized due to debts. Haidušek bought some of the equipment, but there wasn't much.

A few years later I went to Bryan again and hunted for the bound copies of all the printed issues of *Slovan*, the so-called "file." At *Slovan*, as with all newspapers, the printed issues are bound in a cover for safekeeping. It is an important memorial for the future. *Slovan* was the first Texas Czech newspaper, and its file included several volumes that certainly contained important records concerning the history of the Czech settlers in Texas. I thought that someone in Bryan was keeping them, but I couldn't find out anything about them. I went to the county courthouse and searched out the official who had taken part in the confiscation and sale of *Slovan*. When everything valuable had been hauled away, only piles of newsprint remained. They were hauled to an empty lot and burned. Surely the *Slovan* file was taken along with the rest of it, though Haidušek, or whoever it was, could have easily saved it.

I worked for Škarda for a little over a year, but his business began to decline. I found out that they were looking for cigar makers in Austin. I went there and found work wrapping cigars, which paid well. So I got to see the capital of Texas. My son had already learned quite a lot about

4. The RVOS later became known in English as the Farmers Mutual Protective Association of Texas.

cigar making in Boston, and then he had worked at *Slovan;* in Austin, too, he soon found a job.

We were doing well there. But there I found out how women were always being underpaid. My wife went to the same cigar factory that I did. Three other cigar makers were employed there. Saturday was payday, and my wife found less pay than she expected. When I asked the boss about it, he told me that women work for less pay than men everywhere. For exactly the same cigars, a man received seven dollars per thousand, but a woman was paid only five dollars. My wife didn't work there any longer. I established my own factory and became an independent producer.

I began corresponding with several northern newspapers, without pay, of course. An agent for the Geringer newspapers, Volenský, visited me once and told me that if I wanted to write for *Svornost* I would be paid. I think that was in 1890. Up until that time, not only had I not gotten a cent for writing to newspapers, I even had to pay for the newspapers I received. I had never written for a Geringer newspaper, and now I was to be paid for it and get my paper free, too. Naturally, I seized the opportunity, and since that time I have been a continuous correspondent to *Svornost.* Altogether, for over forty years. Other newspapers to which I have subscribed, with the exception of the *New Yorkské Listy,* are dead, but Geringer's publications are still alive.

In Texas I was always being invited to speak at celebrations in Czech communities, where I found customers for my cigars. Many people came to visit us, too. In Austin there is a sanatorium, an institution for the deaf, dumb, and blind, and visiting countrymen who had someone in there usually came to ask me to serve as an interpreter. Almost all of them stayed overnight, or even longer. Also, when women who were ill or who had sick children came to see a doctor, my daughter often went with them to act as an interpreter. Some of our visitors returned our favor by sending us meat, butter, and liver sausage, but there wasn't much of that.

One "well-to-do" farmer with a sick wife stayed with us for three or four days. I went with them to the doctor because neither of them knew English. As they were leaving, they asked what they owed us. I said "nothing," but that he might remember us and send us some butter or other type of food that we have to buy.

We had a Polish neighbor, a country businessman, who traveled around the same part of the country that these people were from, and they could send whatever they wanted to give by him. For a long time nothing came, but in the heat of the summer, he brought butter in a half-gallon can. Of course farmers didn't have ice then, and, in the summer, butter became slushy and had a bad taste, so it couldn't be used. When he could sell butter in cool weather, he hadn't sent anything because he could turn it into money. So my wife threw it out. That was the sort of thanks we often got.

I often wrote to *Svornost* about schools, and I urged our countrymen to get an education. In Austin there was a certain Němec who had a school in which a person could acquire at least a partial education. About six Czech young people enrolled in that school one year. They got together at our house and two marriages resulted, both in Ennis. If they hadn't attended that school they would never in their lives have met.

At that time, a summer excursionary train ran from Austin to San Antonio on Sundays. It left Austin at seven o'clock in the morning and got to San Antonio after eight o'clock. In the evening, it left San Antonio at seven o'clock.

I think that a round-trip ticket cost about two dollars. I took advantage of that train several times and went to San Antonio to see countryman Kříž. He had a saloon and a big hall; he was a good Czech, but he had a German wife, so his kids didn't know Czech. His son had a theater which was called the Krish Opera House; later it lost that name. In San Antonio I met two other countrymen whose names I don't remember, but one was a fireman, and the other worked in the German Turnhalle.

Perhaps the oldest Czech in Texas had been Dignovitý, a native of Kutná Hora.[5] He had said he was a doctor, but Kříž told me that he had been a mill worker in Kutná Hora. In San Antonio he had run a land business and had been convicted of some kind of fraud, they say. That was before the Civil War, and he had said he was innocent, claiming that he was persecuted because he sympathized with the North. During one of my trips to San Antonio, I visited Dignovitý's widow. She was an American, not knowing any language other than English, but she knew Czech history very well. She told me all about the things her husband used to say about Hus and the Taborites, and she was able to pronounce the name Žižka very well.[6]

That was at the beginning of the 1890s when I went to San Antonio and found only three Czechs there. Now there is a lodge of the Texaská Jednota and the Sokol.[7] I visited the Alamo several times, and it appeared as it did when the Texas revolutionaries were slaughtered there.

5. L. W. Dongres mentions Anthony M. Dignovitý in the epilogue, this volume.

6. Jan Žižka was a ruthless but brilliant Czech military commander during the Hussite Wars in the fifteenth century.

7. Jednota probably refers to the largest Czech fraternal organization in Texas, the Slovanská podporující jednota státu Texas (SPJST). The Sokol (Falcon) Society was founded in Prague in 1862

Only now have they gone about buying the surrounding area and turning it into a park.

From Austin we moved to Taylor. Countryman Bartoš got me to go there. He wanted to establish a saloon, and since he felt that I had better appeal as a host than he did, he offered me a partnership. I didn't have any money to put into a business, so he volunteered to pay for it all himself. But the saloon in Taylor turned out to be like the two others in New York.[8] Large fees for licenses, high rent, and small profit. In addition, you're trapped in the place from six in the morning until midnight, sometimes, and that's neither pleasant nor healthy. I held out for perhaps five months. The saloon, like most others, was also a brewery. We passed it on to other partners, and we left. Bartoš moved to Caldwell, where he had a married son and daughter. I didn't lose anything in the saloon business but had neglected my cigar business. Bartoš later opened a saloon in Granger and did well.

I settled in Caldwell and again turned to cigars, which I began to sell in Czech settlements as I had before. In 1898 I received a letter from the publisher of *New Yorské Listy,* asking if I would take over the editor's job. I didn't want to do it, but my wife talked me into it. New York had been our home for twelve years, we had many friends and acquaintances there, and it was more cheerful than the Texas countryside. I agreed. That was in June. I set out on the road again by myself. My wife had to process the leftover tobacco, sell out the cigars, and close down

and has always been known for its gymnastic program. The American branch of the Sokol became one of the most popular Czech-American organizations, although it was not organized in Texas until 1908.

8. Buňata is referring to incidents that he described in an earlier autobiographical article for *Amerikán národní kalendář.*

the workshop in which our son and daughter were helpers.

I was making twelve dollars a week again at *New Yorkské Listy*. When my wife was already preparing for the trip, it occurred to me that twelve dollars a week for an editor was too low, so I asked for fifteen dollars a week. The chief then let me know that they had another person who wanted to do it for twelve dollars and that I was out of a job. I wanted to go back to Caldwell, but my wife had already written me that she had everything ready for the trip and she was leaving. She came, and we went back to producing cigars. . . . [9]

9. Buňata goes on to further describe his itinerant life. After leaving New York City once again, he divided his time between Texas and the Midwest but lived out his final years in Ennis, Texas, where he died in 1934.

EPILOGUE: *L. W. Dongres*

As a Czech-American journalist from the Midwest (like
Buňata), Ludvík W. Dongres brought a fresh perspective to the Texas Czechs. He may be considered a "main-
stream" (Bohemian) Czech American who received his
first taste of the unique Texas Czech culture in 1893
when he visited the state as a reporter for the journal
Hospodář, which at that time was published in Omaha,
Nebraska. (In 1961, *Hospodář* moved to West, Texas,
where it is still being published today.) Although Dongres is more concerned with describing his observations
about Czech life in Texas than in reporting details from
his own life, this first-person account does contain personal anecdotes and it reflects his inquisitive but sympathetic personality very well. Because of its overview
of life among the Czechs in Texas, this essay gives the
reader valuable insights into Czech ethnicity in Texas.
Although the first group of Czech immigrants was composed primarily of Protestants from the Landškroun
region of Bohemia, the majority of Czech immigrants
after the Civil War were Moravian — and Catholic. Today, the term *Czech* is almost universally accepted as
a generic term by Texans whose descendants came from
the geographical region of Moravia, but resistance to
the term *Bohemian* is widespread, with good reason,

and Dongres helps explain why. The reader also learns many historical details from Dongres's inquiries about the Texas Czechs.

Dongres's journalistic background is important to his essay in two ways. First, most of his generalizations about the Texas Czechs—for example, the relative proportions of Catholics, Protestants, and Freethinkers—seem to be objective and accurate, with the exceptions pointed out in the notes. His attempt to be evenhanded (a trait not always shared by other Czech-American journalists of the nineteenth century) in dealing with various groups and factions is obvious. Second, his style, as that of a professional writer, is well developed and readable. His Czech is clear, concise, and relatively easy to translate.

During his career, Dongres interviewed various old Czech settlers in Texas and published their stories in the *Amerikán národní kalendář.* Two examples, those of Mr. and Mrs. Jirásek and Jan Horák, appear in this volume. Dongres's personal essay was originally published in the 1924 *kalendář.*

IN SCHOOLS IN THE OLD COUNTRY WE WERE taught that the western Slavs were called the Czech Slavs and were composed of the Czechs from Bohemia, the Moravians from Moravia, and the Silesians from Silesia, but that the differences among them were only ethnographic—all of them were really Czechs.

Such a theory would serve a person poorly here in Texas. I recognized that immediately in 1893, when Jan Rosický, the publisher of *Hospodář,* for whom I was working as an editor, sent me to Texas on a short trip to find out about farming in the American South. As I was riding my horse up to a farm somewhere in Fayette County, I called to a

L. W. Dongres.
Photograph reproduced from
the *Amerikán národní kalendář* for 1924.

woman who was working in a garden by the side of the road; I guessed that she was a fellow Czech. "Good morning, Mother.[1] Can you tell me if any Czechs live around here?"[2]

"Good morning," came the reply. "Only Moravians live here, but look," she said, pointing toward the Colorado River, "about four miles from us in the river bottom lives a Czech who came here from up North."

"And where is your husband, Mother?"

"Na poli. Sázija s ogary kobzole."[3]

Enthusiastic to learn about this "*kobzole*" plant, of which I had never heard, and anxious to see how one plants "*s ogary*," I got off my horse and joined the farmers in the field. There I found out that *kobzole* were ordinary potatoes and that *ogaři* are—boys.

Countrymen from Moravia compose perhaps 80 percent of our immigrants in Texas and it is certainly true that a majority of them are from eastern Moravia and from the Silesian border in northern Moravia. They have resisted and still resist using the term *Czech;* among themselves they use the term *Moravian.* That even applies to the older members of the second generation in no less degree.

Also, local dialects are preserved. A Hanák and his children, born here, speak Hanák, a Valach, Valachian, and

---

1. Dongres uses the Czech *maminka,* which would be generally appropriate in addressing an unknown, middle-aged lady. An older lady might be addressed as "grandmother" (*babička* in the Bohemian dialects, *stařenka* in the Moravian dialects).

2. The distinction between *Czech* and *Moravian,* a crucial point in Dongres's essay, is actually more confusing in the Czech language than it is in English. In Czech a *Čech* is a native of *Čechy* (Bohemia), but the term is also applied generically to any of the Czech-speaking regions.

3. These sentences, given in Moravian dialect, mean "In the field. He's planting potatoes with the boys."

so forth.[4] Speak to a native of Valašsko about a brick kiln (*cihelna*) and a brick (*cihla*), and he will *surely,* during the course of the conversation, always pronounce the words *tíhle* and not *cihly, tíhelna* and not *cihelna*.

Our people in Texas, even the second and third generations, read and write Moravian,[5] they take Moravian newspapers, and they attend Moravian churches where a Moravian priest gives a Moravian sermon. In their organizations they happily sing "Kde Domov Můj,"[6] but you come to feel their full strength, enthusiasm, and love for their homeland when they sing "I am a Moravian—that is my pride." Even old Mr. Haidušek himself, in his newspaper *Svoboda,* often argued, and quite logically, that just as a Slav born in Bohemia cannot be called a Moravian, a Slav born in Moravia cannot be, and should not be, called a Czech.

The Bohemians[7] who come to settle in Texas in a short time start using the sweet-sounding *tož* (well) and *včil* (now),[8] and their children soon are speaking Moravian.

Not long ago my daughter asked me, "How is it that the *okůrky* that we eat at home are exactly the same as the *oharky* that we have at Grandmother's (at Grandfather and Grandmother's farm)?"[9]

4. Haná and Valachia (Valašsko) are geographical regions within Moravia.

5. Dongres illustrates the use of these dialects by incorporating the Moravian *čne* (reads) and *pše* (writes) into his own sentence.

6. "Kde domov můj" ("Where Is My Home?") is the Czech national anthem.

7. As explained in note 2, *Čech* as used by Dongres is ambiguous, but here it is translated to mean *a native of Bohemia* rather than the English *Czech*.

8. The words in the Bohemian dialects are *tak* and *ted',* respectively.

9. The words *okůrky* (Bohemian) and *oharky* (Moravian) both mean *cucumbers*.

The ethnologists should add the Texas Moravians as a truly distinctive type to the divisions of our Czech nation. Even travelers who stay for very long among our people in Texas come to recognize this. Vojta Beneš always spoke enthusiastically about the Texas Moravians. Conditions in this state add still other distinctive characteristics to the Moravian ones but do not detract from the original qualities of open sincerity and geniality.

The various causes of this phenomenon are not at all due to any kind of opposition or hatred toward the Czechs and mainly relate to the early days of settlement of our people in Texas.

The first families who settled in Texas in the 1850s were from Bohemia, but they were of the Evangelical confession and called themselves "Moravian Brethren." That denomination was well known to Americans by the name "Moravians" and, as such, they received a better welcome from the native inhabitants than the unwelcome "Bohemians," whom the Americans could not, and in large part to this day cannot, distinguish from Gypsies.

The old teacher Josef Holec in his memoirs, in 1885, wrote: "When we arrived early in the spring of 1855 in the town of Cat Spring, there were already about ten Czech, three Moravian, and ten German families settled there." When more immigrants came, almost exclusively from Moravia, the term *Moravian* came into general use, even among the Americans, and our people stuck to it exclusively because it sounded better than *Bohemian* here.

Čapek and Dr. Habenicht have explained why the main flow of immigration from Moravia was turned toward Texas in this way.[10]

---

10. In a note Dongres refers to Tomáš Čapek, *The Čechs (Bohemians) in America;* Jan Habenicht, *Dějiny Čechův Amerických;* and

Before the Austro-Prussian War, Austria was the dominant member of the *Bund* of German states, and Austrian
regiments were garrisoned together with German ones in
various forts in Germany, mainly in Mainz. Before 1848,
a strong emigration movement to Texas prevailed in Germany. It seems more than likely that Lutheran German
soldiers maintained friendly relations with Evangelicals
serving in the Austrian regiments, and that is how it came
about that our first immigrants were Evangelicals. Pastor
Arnošt Bergman began the process in 1848. (Born in 1797
in Zápudov, near Mnichovo Hradiště in Bohemia, he
studied theology in Prussia and then served as pastor of
an Evangelical church in Stroužný, Prussian Silesia). Bergman, who was more German than Czech,[11] came to America in 1848 and settled in Cat Spring, Austin County. From
there he wrote his coreligionists in Bohemia and Moravia
enthusiastic letters about American freedom and the prom-
ising future that the state of Texas afforded immigrants.
In 1850 a certain Václav Matějovský came after him, and
in 1852 a whole group of Evangelical families from around
Landškroun came under the leadership of Josef Šiller.
Among them was Josef Lešikar,[12] the founder of a very

Kenneth D. Miller, "Bohemians in Texas," *Bohemian Review* 4 (May,
1917): 4–5. He also refers to an obscure work by Josef Holec entitled
"Vývin českého školství v Texas" ("The Development of Czech
Schools in Texas"; 1855) and an undated brochure by F. J. Pešek
entitled *Vývin českého školství v okresu Fayette* (Development of
Czech Schools in Fayette County), which was published by the newspaper *Svoboda* in La Grange, Texas.

11. This statement may be misleading; Bergman's nationality is
problematic. See Machann and Mendl, *Krásná Amerika,* pp. 26–28,
226.

12. Dongres is slightly confused in his account here. The group
led by Josef Šilar did reach Cat Spring in the spring of 1852, but
Lešikar's group came separately, arriving in late 1853.

extensive family of Lešikars in Texas. His son Vincenc still lives in Caldwell.[13]

It is not my desire to write a history of Czech immigration to Texas in this almanac, but only to gather material that might be used for one. In Habenicht's history there is an essay devoted to Texas, a very thorough one, for he used notes and materials lent to him by old Mr. Haidušek, who had gathered them during many years of work. (Mr. Haidušek was well suited to the task. He came to Texas in 1856. He was a teacher, a judge, a representative in the state legislature, one of the oldest Czech lawyers in America, and, since 1885, the publisher and editor of the weekly *Svoboda* in La Grange.)

There are, however, several unclear or problematical points in the published histories which I will try to clear up consecutively here in the almanac. I asked Mr. Ed Batla, the county clerk in Austin County, to find for me in the county records which countrymen first owned land there, in the county where the village of Cat Spring is located. Mr. Batla found in the deed book that John Zvolánek (a Protestant minister who came soon after Bergman) bought real estate in 1855 and that in the same year Dr. Anton Hanka (a Czech-German) did as well. In addition, the deed book in Bellville revealed a "Professor E. Bergman." He bought some property in 1856. Also buying land in 1856 was Thomas Batla (the grandfather of the present county clerk, Mr. E. Batla).

One reliable source of information is the book that records the names of those who applied for citizenship and gives the dates of their arrival in the United States. It is in the county seat, and it shows these names: Mathias

---

13. At this point Dongres adds a parenthetical statement: "In the next issue of the almanac, I'll give his biography."

Kuna, 1852; Thomas Batla, 1853; Karel Lešikar, Josef Lešikar, and John Wotipka, all in 1853. Jan Zvolánek, John
Reymershoffer, Josef Rypl, Josef Shiller, and Vincenc Shiller
gave 1854 as the date of their arrival. In 1855, John Wrlla,
Anton Štupl, Thomas Chupík, John Waleček, John Ustyník, Josef Mikeska, Petr Mikeska, and John Zapalač all
arrived.[14]

With the same request, I turned to Mr. Albert F. Mach,
the county clerk of neighboring Fayette County, where almost all of the first immigrants went from their gathering
point in Cat Spring. Mr. Mach informed me that the first
transfer of property to a countryman registered in that
county was as follows: on the 6th of December, 1856, Jiří
Mužný bought forty acres near eastern Navidad Creek
from Ed. Brookfield and paid three dollars an acre for it.
This property now has a value of about one hundred dollars an acre. "It's possible," Mr. Mach wrote me, "that
some countrymen bought earlier, but in the deed records
of Fayette County, Jiří Mužný is recorded as the first." In
1859 the first countrymen requesting citizenship were Valentin Haidušek, Valentin Holub, František Marak, Ignác
Šrámek, Frank Kosa, František and Josef Horák, Matěj
Novák, Josef Janda, and Ignác Mužný. The majority of
these came in 1856 in the month of August as part of a
larger wave of an immigration expedition from around
Frenštát in Moravia. However, those requesting citizenship papers were issued them only after the Civil War, in
1866, in the January session of the county court in La
Grange.

14. It is common in studying records of the time to find the Czech
and English forms of given names (Jan/John, Josef/Joseph, Petr/
Peter) used interchangeably, sometimes even in reference to the same
person.

Dr. Antonín Dignovitý, generally considered to be the first countryman to settle in Texas, came to New York in 1832 and to Texas at the beginning of the late 1840s. He settled in San Antonio, where he had a medical practice, although he had been trained in Europe as an engineer. (Dr. Habenicht says that he studied medicine in a college in Cincinnati, Ohio.) Dr. Dignovitý left Texas in 1850, however, and led an adventurous life in the "Wild West." In 1842 he married an American in Little Rock, Arkansas, and in 1856 returned to San Antonio, where he died in 1875 at the age of sixty-five. He had no influence on Czech immigration to Texas because he lived separated from his countrymen, and his descendants do not acknowledge their Slavic origin, even though (according to Čapek) in 1888, his son A. F. Dignovitý advertised, in *Pokrok Západu*,[15] extensive lands in Kinney, Texas, for a Czech colony that did not come about. Old Dignovitý was a real Czech and a patriot. He wrote and, in 1859, published in New York a brochure in English, *Bohemia under Austrian Despotism*.[16]

The total number of our people in Texas is uncertain, but I believe that the figure of fifty thousand is the best estimate. Of this number, about 80 percent are Catholic. Texas has more Czech Catholic parishes than any state in the Union. About 15 percent of the population claim to be Protestants (mostly Czech-Moravian Brethren), and the remaining 5 percent are Freethinkers. I am counting only those among them who are wholehearted Freethinkers, and I estimate this number from the membership of

15. This was a Czech-language newspaper published in Omaha by Jan Rosický, the man for whom Dongres had been working. The name means "Progress of the West."

16. Dignovitý's *Bohemia under Austrian Despotism,* despite its title, is an autobiography and is a book of substantial length.

ČSPS in this state, an additional eight "Freethinker communities," and a handful of active Freethinkers gathered
around "Freethought." The SPJST has more members than
all the other Czech fraternal associations in Texas together.[17] Catholic, Brethren, and even Freethinking countrymen belong to it.

Probably the first Czech organization was the "Czech
Reading Society," founded in 1869 in the Evangelical community of Wesley in Washington County. A year later, the
Evangelical countrymen in Ross Prairie, near Fayetteville,
formed an association called "Enlightenment," which
maintained a Czech school. The first Catholic organization was formed after the arrival of the first Czech priest
in 1872. He was Rev. Josef Chromčík, born in 1845 in Řep-
čín, near Olomouc, a patriotic priest who is remembered
for this piety, not only by his coreligionists but by all of
the countrymen who came into contact with him, exactly
like the first Evangelical priests Opočenský and Juren and
the late leader of Texas Freethinkers, Ant. Kulhánek. The
first lodge admitted to the ČSPS was the "Texan" lodge in
Praha, Lavaca County. It was dedicated by Mr. Kirchman
from Chicago, who, on the next day, dedicated the second lodge, "Čechomoravan,"[18] in Ellinger.

When the inevitable moment finally comes and the last
Czech completely disappears in the American melting pot

17. The full title of the organization is the Slovanská podporující
jednota státu Texas (the Slovanic Benevolent Society of the State of
Texas), which actually began as an offshoot of the national ČSPS
(Česko-slovanský podporující spolek, or the Czech-Slovanic Benevolent Society). Although ČSPS was oriented in the Freethought movement, the SPJST was much more moderate, as Dongres implies.
Nevertheless, Czech Catholics in Texas formed their own fraternal
groups.
18. *Čechomoravan* means *Czech-Moravian.*

made up of all the nations of the world, I predict that the last Czech-American "Mohican" will be from Texas.[19]

You in the North worry yourselves silly over our third generation, which is slipping away from us and disappearing into cast-iron, 100-percent Americanism faster than camphor into air. We in Texas are not upset about this. First of all, nothing can be done about it; secondly, we are one generation ahead over here. We have it better as a result of the special educational situation that the immigrants found here in the 1850s and 1860s.

In the sparsely settled wilderness at that time, there were no schools, and so these first pioneers of ours began to establish schools of their own — Czech, or rather, "Moravian."

That was really the golden age of Czech education in America, in spite of the privation and poverty in which the parents, and to an even greater extent, the teachers of their children lived.

Who was the first Czech teacher in Texas? Various names have been suggested. The former teacher Josef Holec wrote in his memoirs (1885) that when he came to Cat Spring in 1855, ten Czech, three Moravian, and ten German Evangelical families had built a church in which the Czech pastor Bergman taught the children. "What Pastor Bergman taught, I don't know," continues Holec. "I have heard that he taught Germans, among others. Pastor Bergman, even though he was born in Bohemia, was brought up as a German, and even though there is no proof one way or the other, with some difficulty he can be placed among 'Czech' teachers, and in that case, the priority would belong to

19. Dongres's allusion is to James Fenimore Cooper's novel *The Last of the Mohicans;* two of its central characters are the last remaining members of an American Indian tribe.

him." Holec went on to write about him: "Unable to make a living from either teaching or teaching and preaching combined, he planted a vineyard, raised corn, and dispensed medicinal herbs and medical advice to people. He often rode over twenty miles to plow the land in order to make a living. There were few children, and even fewer were sent to school — and the salary, although small, was not paid the teacher." It seems more likely that Pastor Jos. J. Zvolánek, who came to Cat Spring soon after Bergman and even preached in Czech in the local Evangelical church, taught the Czech children in their native language. But there is no proof of that, either.

It is absolutely certain, though, that the first real teacher of a Czech school in Texas was Josef Mašík. He had already been a teacher in Bohemia, having studied pedagogy under his tutor Jan Ženatý, the teacher in Jimravov. Mašík passed the teachers' examinations which were required in Austria at that time (1826) and became a student teacher in Březina u Svratky, and then in Čermná u Landškrouna. He participated in the revolutionary movement of 1848 and stood in the forefront of the deputation of teachers who passed through Olomouc before that Viennese revolution of Franz-Josef's popped up, asking for an improvement in teachers' pay. In 1854, Mašík and his family set out on the road to Texas. His wife died of cholera on the way, and he and his three children had to work for a German on a ranch near Cat Spring for five dollars a month.

Then he took up farming, but because of poor crops he constantly fell into greater debt. In 1859, he began to teach a regular daily Czech school which had been founded by the Czech Reading Society in Wesley, Washington County, about twenty miles from Cat Spring. He taught there for thirteen years and retired at the age of sixty-two in 1872. F. B. Zdrůbek came after him.

The second professional teacher was F. J. Pešek, born in 1850 near Netolice in Bohemia. He studied to be a teacher in the German schools in Budějovice, and in 1867, fearing he would be drafted, came to America. In 1868 he began to privately teach the children of Czech parents in the empty home of Ignác Šrámek near Mulberry, Fayette County.

In 1864 Miss Holubová taught in Czech at the Haidušek home and in 1868 the widow Kubalová taught in her home in Bluff. During the Civil War, Czech schools almost disappeared.

In 1867 Alois Koňakovský taught in cabins where black slaves had formerly lived on the farm of Jan Wychopeň near Fayetteville. Koňakovský, who came from the Old Country, was well educated and a painter of unusual talent. . . .[20]

After Koňakovský, Josef Křenek taught in the home of Josef Janák in Ross Prairie, but only for a few months in 1870. A real Czech school was erected there already by 1871 (the building measuring twenty feet by twenty feet), and the first teacher was Josef Holec. Also, according to [Tomáš] Hruška, Anna Velčovská was one of the first Czech teachers. The life of a Czech teacher in Texas was full of hardship, privation, and poverty. Holec complained about these conditions in the following jeremiad:

It was a hard beginning for those schools. There weren't any primers or any other books, and as

20. At this point Dongres refers to a reproduction of a painting (depicting the earliest Czech wedding in Texas) which accompanied his *kalendář* article, and he goes on to remark on the fact that Texas Czechs commonly refer to a painting and a photograph by the same term: *malování*. See Machann and Mendl, *Krásná Amerika*, p. 147, for a reproduction of the painting.

soon as a student learned to read and write a little, he had to stay at home and work. Koňakovský used *Slavie* as his only educational aid.[21] In 1872 the Jonáš brothers published a small primer (through the publishers of *Slavie*) and, a year later, a larger one of forty pages. August Geringer published a larger primer in 1875, a second reader in the next year, and then a history of the Union. In 1879 a primer and a reader were published for Catholic schools. And as it was with books, so it was with teachers. Just as Bergman from Cat Spring, in order to make a living, had to look outside school for his daily bread, so it was also for Křenek, Koňakovský, Kubalová, and others too. I myself used to chop cotton in the morning before it was time to go to school. And when I let the children go home, I started out with my hoe again, if I wanted to eat supper. I planted and sold tobacco so that I could buy a coat and shoes.

From the above account it would seem as if the State of Texas really did not care at all about the education of its people. But that was not the case. It is true that our public schools, mainly in the rural districts, as in all the slave states, even today remain far behind those in the North. But even so, public schools or, as they say, "state" schools, were founded wherever there were enough inhabitants in the district and the people wanted a school. In such schools, the state paid the teacher for three or four months a year. Until 1871, there was no required inspection of the schools and, also, the law did not require any

21. This was a Czech-language newspaper published in Racine, Wisconsin.

particular language as the medium of instruction in either the community or state schools.

The first Czech families that settled in the community of Ross Prairie had a state school there. Mrs. Simpson, the American teacher, taught only in English, of course, so our people did not send their children to public school. Only the Hajdušek children went to school there; they learned English and received an American education.[22]

Where our people made up the majority, a Czech teacher was obtained for the state school. Of course he did not know English, and so he taught only in "Moravian." Where there were more Germans, teaching was in German or "in both languages." (This can explain the Germanization of some early Moravian families. Otherwise, the Moravians and Germans here always have had a most friendly relationship, including intermarriage, and, in addition, many of our people, even national leaders, are to this day members of the German fraternal organization "Sons of Hermann.")

Old man Ječmenek told me about a teacher who had been teaching at the public state school in their community for several years when he was called to court as a witness. He had to use an interpreter because he did not know a word of English. The Moravian immigrants in Texas long have felt that it is a duty to maintain their national identity by preserving their language, and so they have not wanted to send their children to English-language schools. May it be stated to the honor of old Hajdušek that he always spoke out against this and that he encouraged his countrymen to care about the American education of their children. Because of the bad laws during this period, one can find many people in Texas who are already old and

22. The name is usually spelled *Haidušek*.

were born here, and yet who do not know English at all. There was a time in Czech communities when you could not converse in any language other than Czech.

Even four years ago, when I was the editor of the local English newspaper in Sealy, Texas, a countryman who was older than I came to me and asked me to stop sending him the paper.

"I only know how to read Moravian. I don't know English."

"Did you recently come from Europe?"

"I was born here, but our teacher was a Moravian, so we weren't able to learn English."

In 1893, when I got off the train in Fayetteville, a black man, as black as if he had just arrived from Zulu-Kafer, grabbed my traveling bags and said in fluent Moravian, "I'll take your bags for you."

I looked at him with wide eyes, and perhaps my mouth fell open, for the Negro flashed a white-toothed smile at me and said, "I'm a black Moravian, a black son of a bitch."

There were several black families there whose adult children spoke Moravian better than English.

In 1871, a law was passed that disqualified anyone who had not passed a test in the English language from teaching in the public schools. The Czech teachers who did not know English well enough had to give up their jobs, although several "slipped through the back door." In places where the school was composed of two or more classes, the test was required only of the principal or the headmaster, and the other teachers were exempt.

This situation did not last long, however, and later, a law was passed that required that the language of instruction in all schools — state, parochial, and private — must be English. However, courses other than those prescribed by the state plan for all schools may be taught in any language.

In Texas today there are no independent Czech schools, at least not like those maintained by Czech groups in the northern states and educational sponsors in larger cities.

Why? The desire is great, but conditions will not allow it. This would be hard to explain to anyone who does not understand how the South is dominated by the cotton industry.

In twenty-seven Czech Catholic communities in Texas, they have so-called community schools, attended by several thousand Czech children. (Some schools have over three hundred children.) But the language of instruction must be English. In the majority of these schools, the priests or teaching nuns teach Czech after regular school hours. This is the reason Czech is a required course for Czech students of the college and seminary in La Porte and why one can find a Czech institute for nuns in Shiner.

The Brethren ministers also attempt to fulfill the goal of Czech teachers in Sunday schools, and, in conjunction with the Methodist mission, the Rev. V. Cejnar taught Czech from 1908 and 1911 at Southwestern University.

The Freethinker community, in conjunction with the Sokol in Guy and the SPJST "Štefánik" lodge in Houston, often holds a Czech Sunday school.

In spite of this utter lack of preparatory education in the Czech language, Czech has been taught at the University of Texas since 1915.

The first attempt to introduce Czech as a course of study at the University of Texas came in 1912. At that time Czech university students C. Černoský (lawyer and judge), L. Mikeska and Miloslav Breuer (doctors), K. Křenek, and several others founded the club called "Čechie" and then asked university president Dr. E. Mezes to establish a Czech chair. Their request was turned down because there were not enough Czech students. By 1914 more Czech students had come to the university, and they decided to try again. The petition (which was printed in the student newspaper *The Daily Texan* on May 25, 1915) was signed by the following Czech students from various schools of higher learning in the state: E. Mikeska from Baylor University, I. Shiller from Trinity University, J. Migl from San Marcos Normal, Helen Hošková from Denton Normal, and K. Knížek from the state university [University of Texas] and the current chairman of the "Čechie" academic club. Mr. Method Pázdral, a lawyer and a member of the Czech National Council for the State of Texas, was asked for his signature and legal help. Dr. Mezes, the president of the university, promised that he would see to it that Czech was introduced, but only under the condition that a special professor not be asked for. He called upon K. Knížek, who was at the time a senior student serving as an instructor in the Department of Germanic Languages, to teach Czech as well. The credit for this fortuitous decision by Dr. Mezes belongs to Dr. E. Prokeš, who was born a Czech but raised as a German, and who had a strong interest in the "Čechie" club.[23] Dr. Mezes resigned before he could fulfill his promise, and his successor, Dr. W. Battle, was not inclined toward the wishes of the Czech students. Method Pázdral went to Austin when the state legislature was holding hearings on the state university [University of Texas] and appealed directly to the leaders of the legislature. Again, all was in vain. However, the members of "Čechie" did not give up hope and turned to Representatives Blaylock and Burmeister, who had the most Czech

23. Evidently Dr. Prokeš was able to influence Dr. Mezes's decision, but his precise role in this matter is unclear.

voters in their districts. When it came time to vote on the general appropriations bill, these two representatives pushed through an amendment financing an independent Czech department, which later became the Department of Slavic Languages at the University of Texas. Representative Burmeister appealed to the legislature with statements such as this: "You have given over twenty thousand dollars to the French, you've given over twenty thousand to the Germans. What will you give to the Czechs?"[24]

The bill passed on May 24, 1915. K. Knížek was named the teacher, and he is there up to the present day. (I thank him for this information.)

Dr. L. Mikeska, Dr. H. Mareš, Dr. R. Mareš, Miss L. Mikesková, Miss L. Škrabánková, Miss L. Marešová, J. Talášek, J. Chupík, J. Tobola, E. Macháček, and Miss A. Mondříková were registered in the Czech department in the first year.

For the eight years that Czech was taught (together with Russian), about one hundred students took courses. The largest number was eighteen, the smallest was six. During the 1922–23 school year, nine were regular students and six were correspondence students. The number of Czech students at the university is small, and many of those who take Czech completely lack a basic knowledge of the language so that the teaching of Czech cannot be at a strict university level.

How times change! Only a short time ago, people who were born in Texas didn't know English, and now their children don't know Czech. Even we in Texas, with whom, it is said, the Czech language will be long preserved, even we have fallen into the melting pot of Americanism, and

---

24. Burmeister was referring to the dollar amounts of the appropriations for teaching French and German at the university.

the strongest heat of nativism, inciting hatred of immigrants, is directed on us from below. In Texas it comes chiefly from the Ku Klux Klan, which, unfortunately, is supported even by some Czech renegades—native Texas Moravians.

Years from now, in Bohemia, when they teach children the ethnographic divisions of the Czechoslovak nation, they will say: "The Bohemians live in Bohemia, the Moravians in Moravia, the Slovaks in Slovakia. In North America there once lived American Czechs, after which came the Czech Americans. In Texas lived the Texas Moravians, who were the last to become extinct."

Bibliographic Note

The standard book-length works on the subject of Czech-American history are still Tomáš Čapek's *Naše Amerika* (Our America) (Prague: Narodní-Rada Československá, 1926) and *Moje Amerika* (My America) (Prague: Fr. Borový, 1935), both published in Prague, Czechoslovakia. Čapek's English-language version, *The Čechs (Bohemians) in America* (Boston: Houghton-Mifflin, 1920) is less complete and definitive but superior to any other English-language work. Čapek had a comprehensive knowledge of Czech-American communities in the Midwest and Northeast; however, he was less familiar with Texas. Jan Habenicht's *Dějiny čechův amerických* (History of the Czechs in America) (St. Louis: Hlas, 1904–10) offers valuable information about the early history of the Czech settlements in Texas which is unavailable elsewhere. Unlike Čapek, who collected every conceivable United States and state government statistic, Habenicht relies more on personal observation and information from his informants. Both Habenicht and Čapek are interesting for their extensive personal contacts, however.

In many ways, *Naše dějiny* (Our History) (Granger, Tex., 1939), compiled by the National Council of Czech Catholics in Texas, is the most comprehensive work on the history of Texas Czech communities. Unfortunately, the important minority of non-Catholic Czechs in Texas is slighted, although not entirely ignored. Estelle Hudson and Henry R. Maresh's *Czech Pioneers of the Southwest* (Dallas: South-West Press, 1934) provided much valuable anecdotal information in an attempt to cover the entire Texas Czech community, but it is uneven in its treatment and disorganized. William Phillip Hewitt's 1978 dissertation at the University of Texas, "The Czechs in Texas: A Study of the Immigration and the Development of Czech Ethnicity, 1850–1920," provides an excellent account of early immigration and settlement and is well documented. *The Czechs in Texas: A Symposium* (College Station: Texas A&M University, College of Liberal Arts, and Texas Committee for the Humanities, 1979), edited by Clinton Machann, provided new information on a variety of subjects related to the Texas Czechs, but it, like other major sources, was not readily available to readers and scholars. *Krásná Amerika: A Study of the Texas Czechs, 1851–1939* (Austin: Eakin, 1983) by Clinton Machann and James W. Mendl sought to provide a comprehensive study of the subject and attempted to cover the "Czech-American experience" in Texas from historical, sociological, folkloric, and literary perspectives, with an emphasis on the development of Texas Czech ethnicity up to the time of World War II; but perhaps its main contribution was to suggest additional potentially valuable opportunities for research.

The most complete bibliography of publications about and by Czech-Americans is Esther Jerabek's *Czechs and Slovaks in North America: A Bibliography* (New York: Czechoslovak Society of Arts and Sciences in America and Czechoslovak National Council of America, 1976). This work, for the most part, supersedes Tomáš Čapek's *Padesát let českého tisku v Americe od vydání "Slowana amerikanského" v Racine, dne 1. ledna 1860, do 1. ledna 1910* (New

York: Bank of America, 1911). The Čapek bibliography is still valuable for its extensive bibliographical essays and annotations, however. The most complete bibliography of works by and about Texas Czechs (including European sources) is contained in *Krásná Amerika*. The following list of books and pamphlets from the 1980s, compiled with the aid of Robert Janak, is intended as a supplement to that bibliography. In general these items are published by the author or by small presses. Because Czech diacritical markings were omitted or used inconsistently in the original titles, they are omitted here.

Baca, Leo. *Czech Immigration Passenger Lists.* 2 vols. Hallettsville, Tex.: Old Homestead Publishing Co., 1983, 1985.

Barler, Beatrice Ripple. *Marriage Licenses (Issued to Czechs): Austin County.* Bellville, Tex.: By the author, 1981.

———— *The Shiller Family That Came on the Ship "Maria."* Bellville, Tex.: By the author, 1982.

Blaha, Albert J. *Czech Families in Texas from the 1860 Census.* Houston: By the author, 1982.

———— *Czech Families of Fayette County.* 2 vols. Houston: By the author, 1984.

———— *Czech Genealogists' Hand Book.* 4th ed. Houston: By the author, 1986.

———— *Czech Settlements and Families in Texas before 1900.* Houston: By the author, 1983.

———— *Passenger Lists for Galveston.* Vol. 1, 1850–55. Houston: By the author, 1985.

Blaha, Albert J., and Edmond H. Hejl. *Register Records of the Czech-Moravian Brethren: Nelsonville.* Houston: By the authors, 1980.

———— *Register Records of the Czech-Moravian Brethren: Ross Prairie.* Houston: By the authors, 1980.

———— *Register Records of the Czech-Moravian Brethren: Wesley.* Houston: By the authors, 1980.

Blaha, Albert J., and Dorothy Klumpp. *The Saga of Ernst Bergmann*. Houston: By the authors, 1981.

Bujnoch, Dorothy, and Anne Rhodes. *Czech Footprints across Lavaca County, 1860–1900*. Vol. 1. Hallettsville, Tex.: By the authors, 1984.

Cernosek, Donald, and Grace Campbell Clowe. *Czech Marriage Records of Fayette County*. Houston: Albert J. Blaha, 1984.

Clowe, Grace Campbell. *Austin County, Texas. Czech Census Extracts: 1860, 1870, 1880, and 1900*. Albuquerque, N.Mex.: By the author, 1983.

———— *Colorado County, Texas. Czech Census Extracts: 1860, 1870, 1880, and 1900*. Albuquerque, N.Mex.: By the author, 1983.

———— *Czech Extractions from McLennan County, Texas*. Albuquerque, N.Mex.: By the author, 1985.

———— *Czechs in Wesley and Latium, Washington County*. Albuquerque, N.Mex.: By the author, 1985.

———— *Declarations and Marriages of the Czechs in Colorado County*. Albuquerque, N.Mex.: By the author, 1985.

Gloeckner, Annie Mae. *Czechs in Wharton County*. Pierce, Tex.: By the author, 1985.

Hannan, Kevin. *From Silesia to Texas: A History of the Shirocky, Antonczyk and Fojcik Families*. Dallas, Tex.: By the author, 1984.

Hejl, Edmond H. *Villages of Origin (Protestant)*. Fort Worth, Tex.: By the author, 1983.

Janak, Joseph D. Jr. *A Family History of Ondrej and Rosalie Janak's Children — John, Frank, Mikulas, Vincent, Ondrej, Jr., Ignac —Their Ancestors, Journey to America, Settlement in Texas, and Customs, Traditions, Joys and Hardships Endured*. Victoria, Tex.: By the author, 1984.

Janak, Robert. *The Bohemian Connection*. 2nd ed. Hallettsville, Tex.: Old Homestead Publishing Co., 1985.

———— *Dubina, Hostyn and Ammannsville: The Geographic Origin of Three Czech Communities in Fayette County, Texas.* Beaumont, Tex.: By the author, 1978.

———— *Geographic Origin of Czech Texas.* Hallettsville, Tex.: Old Homestead Publishing Co., 1986.

———— *The Mikeska Family of Zadverice.* Vol. 1. Beaumont, Tex.: By the author, 1986.

———— *Old Bohemian Tombstones.* 2 vols. Beaumont, Tex.: By the author, 1983, 1985.

———— *Simicek Sugarek Janak.* Beaumont, Tex.: By the author, 1976.

Labaj, Stacy. *Obituaries of the Czech Moravian Brethren in Texas.* N.p.: Ben A. Merrick and Albert J. Blaha, 1986.

Machann, Clinton, ed. *Papers from Czech Music in Texas: A Sesquicentennial Symposium.* College Station, Tex.: Komenský Press, 1987.

Mesecke, Anjanette, ed. *Proceedings of the Second Czech Symposium.* Temple, Tex.: Temple Junior College, 1983.

Milberger, Olivia, Herbert B. Milberger, Leona Smiga, and Edward Smiga. *The Families of George and Marianna Konarik Cernota.* Victoria, Tex.: By the authors, 1984.

Miller, Dorothy S. *Czech Pioneers in Texas: Vincenc Doubrava and Frantiska Novak Doubrava and Their Descendants.* Bryan, Tex.: Wallace, 1979.

Morkovsky, Alois J. *Short Biographies of Czech and Other Priests in Texas.* Hallettsville, Tex.: By the author, 1982.

Morris, Nick A. *A History of the SPJST: A Texas Chronicle, 1897–1980.* Temple, Tex.: Stillhouse Hollow Publishers, 1984.

Pearce, Julia Ripple. *Czechs in Texas: Generation by Generation from the 1852 Arrival of Ripple Family and the 1856 Arrival of Chovanec Family.* El Campo, Tex.: By the author, 1981.

Sarris, Kay E., and Elizabeth M. Semrad. *The Zvolanek Clan of Yesterday and Today, 1610–1985.* Houston: Albert J. Blaha, 1985.

Skrabanek, Robert L. *We're Czechs.* College Station: Texas A&M University Press, 1988.

Smith, E. F., and James Valigura. *Obituaries from May 1957 to May 1969: Lavaca County Tribune, Halletsville, Texas.* Conroe, Tex.: James Valigura, 1984.

Tise, Sammy. *Lavaca County Texas, Cemetery Records.* 2 vols. Hallettsville, Tex.: By the author, 1983, 1985.

Wright, Jody Feldtman. *Czechs in Grey and Blue, Too!* San Antonio, Tex.: By the author, 1988.

Index

NOTE: In Czech, the feminine form of surnames differs from the masculine (e.g., Zapalač—Zapaločová); however, in this index, when feminine forms are not specifically cited in the text, the names of women are given in the same form as those for men, in the conventional English manner. Surnames are often cited in the text without (or with abbreviated) given names; in addition, a few surnames are cited in two or more variant forms. For these reasons, it is possible that some individuals who could not be positively identified are indexed in more than one entry.

Index

Battle of San Jacinto, xv
Baylor County, 93
Baylor University, 131
Beaumont, 47
Bedeker, _____, 15
Bednář, _____, 67
Bell County, xix, 75, 93
Belleville, 62
Bellville, 45, 52, 120
Belton, 75
Beneš, Vojta, 118
Bergman, Rev. Arnošt (Ernst),
xv, xvi, xxi, 3, 13, 14, 119–20,
124–25, 127
Bethany, J. W., 64, 65
Bezecný, Fr., 82
Big Elm, 68
Bill, Box, 30
Blaylock, Rep., 131
Blažek, Frank, 97
Blažek, Jindřich, 97
Blažek, Josef, xiv, xix, xxi, xxiv,
95–99
Blažek, Josefina, 97
Blažek, Marie, 97
Bluff, xxi, 126
Blumauer, Johann Aloys, 10
Bohemia, xvi, xvii
Bolden, Col. J., 67
Borovský, Karel Havlíček, 12,
13n
Bosque County, 74
Boston, 101, 103, 104, 108
Branecký, František, xiv, xvii,
xix, xxiii, xxvii, 33–38
Brazos County, xix, 75, 97
Brazos River, 28, 74
Brazos Santiago, 58
Bremen, 15, 34, 79
Brenham, 20, 64
Breuer, Dr. Miloslav, 130
Březina u Svratky, 125
Březnice, xxiv, 40
Bridgeport, 104
Brno, 8
Brookfield, Ed., 121
Brownsville, 80

Bryan, 103, 104, 106, 107
Budějovice, 126
Buňata, Josef, xii, xiv, xxix,
xxixn, xxx, 98, 100–12, 113
Buňata, Mrs. Josef, 101–12
    passim
Burleson County, xix, 88
Burmeisteer, Rep., 131, 132

Čada, Josef S., 100, 101, 103,
106
Cairo, Ill., 61, 62
Caldwell, 92, 93, 111, 112
Camp Gross, 47
Camp Moore, 82
Čapek, Tomáš, xxvn, xxvin,
100, 118, 122
Cat Spring, xv, xvi, xvii, xxi, 3,
13, 18, 28, 34, 35, 42, 44, 45,
63, 80, 118, 119, 120, 121, 124,
125, 127
Čechie, 130, 131
Cejnar, Rev. V., 130
Čermenský u Landškrouna, 7
Čermi, 89, 91
Čermná, xvi, 64, 125
Černoský, C., 130
Česká Třebová, 11, 12
Česko-Bratrský Hlasatel, 12
Česko-slovanský hospodářský
spolek, 97, 98
Česko-slovanský podporující
spolek. *See* ČSPS
Český Dobříš, 84
Chicago, xii, xxv, 123
Childers, Thomas C., xviii
Chlumský, Rev., 92
Chotek, Hugo, 98
Chromčík, Rev. Josef, 123
Chrudí, 12
Chrudim County, 89
Chupík, J., 132
Chupík, Thomas, 121
Cincinnati, 122
Cleburne, 69
Cleveland, 104
Cole, Ar., 64

Index

Marak, František, 121
Marčák, Jos., 89
Marek, Josef, 89
Marek, Josefina, xxiv, 98
Marek, Vinc., 89
Mareš, Anna, 91
Mareš, Josef, 91
Mareš, Dr. R., 132
Maresh (Mareš), Dr. Henry R.,
    4, 132
Marešová, L., 132
Mašek, J., 48
Mašík, Josef, xxi, 28, 68, 91, 92,
    125
Mašík, L., 75
Matamoros, 56, 57, 58, 85, 86
Matějovský, Václav, 119
Maximilian, Emperor of Mex-
    ico, xvn, xviii, 84, 85
"Memoirs of Czech Settlers in
    America," xii
Menzl, Bohumir, xv
Mexico, xviii, 18, 20, 21, 22, 29,
    30, 37, 51, 52, 55–58, 63, 82,
    84–87 passim
Mexico City, 85
Mezes, Dr. E., 130, 131
Migl, J., 131
Mikeska, _____, 93
Mikeska, Dr. L., 93, 130, 131
Mikeska, E., 131
Mikeska, Jan, 42
Mikeska, Josef, 42, 121
Mikeska, Petr, 42, 64, 121
Mikesková, L., 132
Millheim, 35, 42, 45
Mississippi, 20, 52
Mississippi River, 60, 61
Missouri, 82
Mnichovo Hradiště, 119
Modrý, 8
Mondříková, A., 132
Montague County, 67, 68
Monterrey, 86, 87
Moravian Brethren, 118
Moravské noviny, 12, 15
Mottl, Karel, 89

Mulberry, 37, 38, 126
Mustang, 53
Mužný, Ignác, 121
Mužný, Jiří, 121

Nagl, _____, 44
Nagl, Dr., 23
Napajedla, 7
Napoleon, 23
Národní noviny (American), 17,
    18
Národní noviny (European),
    xxiii, 4, 11
Národní svaz českých katolíků v
    Texasu, xxi
Navidad Creek, 121
Nebraska, xxvi, 97
Needville, 83
Nelsonville, 63, 64, 91, 92
Němcová, Božena, 12, 13
Němec, _____, 109
Nepomuky, xvi, 9, 11, 26
Netolice, 126
New Braunfels, xv
New Orleans, xvi, 26, 47, 49,
    50, 58, 60, 82
New Tabor (Nový Tabor), 88,
    92
New Ulm, 15, 91
New York City, xxvi, 103, 104,
    106, 111, 122
New Yorkské Listy, 108, 111,
    112
Nietche, Carolyn, 79
Novák, _____, 37, 38, 87
Novák, Matěj, 121
Nová Osada, 93

Oak Hill, 83
Ohio, 122
Olomouc, 123, 125
Omaha, 113
Opočenský, Rev. Josef, 80, 92,
    123
Orizaba, 85
Ozark Mountains, 82

Index

Czech Voices was composed into type on a Compugraphic digital phototypesetter in eleven point Sabon with three points of spacing between the lines. Sabon was also selected for display. The book was designed by Cameron Poulter, typeset by Metricomp, Inc., printed offset by Thomson-Shore, Inc., and bound by John H. Dekker & Sons, Inc. The paper on which this book is printed carries acid-free characteristics for an effective life of at least three hundred years.

TEXAS A&M UNIVERSITY PRESS : COLLEGE STATION

ISBN 0-89096-846-2

90000

9 780890 968468